The Year
We Had No President

By

RICHARD H. HANSEN

UNIVERSITY OF NEBRASKA PRESS · LINCOLN · 1962

Publishers on the Plains
UNP

233

To Dwight D. Eisenhower

*The first President to take positive
action on presidential disability*

Foreword

The subject of this book is as important as the office of the United States Presidency itself. The constitutional uncertainties of presidential inability cause it to be one of the few areas where there is general agreement among legislators, political scientists, and constitutional lawyers that there is a need for corrective action by constitutional amendment. Nevertheless, no proposed amendment has ever been brought to a vote in either house of the Congress. Since the illnesses of President Eisenhower, no session of Congress has passed without the introduction of one or more proposed amendments dealing with this problem. In 1958 and again in 1959, the Senate Judiciary Subcommittee on Constitutional Amendments favorably reported proposed amendments but no further action was taken.

I do not believe that the failure of Congress to approve a constitutional amendment and present it to the states for ratification is due to indifference or apathy. It is due instead to disagreement and doubt as to the form which a constitutional amendment should take. Any proposal is necessarily a procedure which would divest a duly elected President of the powers of that office. We wrestle with delicate problems touching upon the fundamental principles of separation of powers and the coordinate independence of the separate branches of government. This is all the more reason to continue and step up the quest for a constitutional solution. The demands of the nuclear age upon the office of President require that the discharge of its duties never be in suspension or uncertainty.

As Chairman of the Subcommittee on Constitutional Amendments, I have observed increased interest in this question, but there continues to be wide variation in the approaches taken by those who work for a solution. *The Year We Had No President* is a unique and valuable contribution to the literature of this subject and it should increase public awareness of the implications of this serious constitutional vacuum. The historical, political, and legal analysis which Mr. Hansen has made will certainly be of great assistance to those in government who seek to resolve this issue.

ESTES KEFAUVER, *Chairman*
Subcommittee on Constitutional
Amendments
Committee on the Judiciary
United States Senate

Contents

A picture section follows page 68

The Year We Had No President

Chapter I

The Gap in the Constitution

Thirty-four men have held the office of President of the United States. Pick up any American history, any standard reference work, and you will see their names, starting with George Washington in 1789 and ending with the present incumbent, John Fitzgerald Kennedy, inaugurated on January 20, 1961. The line of presidential succession is consecutive and continuous for the 173 years of this republic's existence. When was the year we had no President?

The year we had no President is the sum total of the periods—hours, days, weeks, even months—when the man in the White House was too sick to be capable of exercising the powers vested in him by the Constitution as Chief Executive and Commander in Chief. These power vacuums —during which for all practical purposes our country had no President—have occurred in seven administrations. The figures are as follows:

William Henry Harrison	Bedridden for 7 days before his death
Zachary Taylor	Bedridden for 5 days before his death
James A. Garfield	Bedridden for 80 days before his death
William McKinley	Bedridden for 8 days before his death
Woodrow Wilson	280 days from his stroke until he resumed cabinet meetings
Warren G. Harding	Semi-invalid for 4 days before his death
Dwight D. Eisenhower	143 days from his heart attack until his announced recovery

Confront the man in the street with this rundown* and

---

*This calendar does not take into account the nine hours and twenty-seven minutes that Abraham Lincoln was unconscious before he died; or the period of Grover Cleveland's incapacity during and after the chances are better than even that his reaction will be: "So what? We've got a Vice President, haven't we?" Like the majority of his fellow citizens, he subscribes to the comforting fallacy that when the President is disabled, the Vice President can step in and act as a sort of substitute President. *But can he?* In 1955 President Eisenhower was stricken by coronary thrombosis. His Vice President, Richard M. Nixon, has written of the ensuing weeks during which "the possibility of an attack on the United States was always hanging over us." If the attack came, nuclear retaliation might be a requisite for survival. *"Would the President be well enough to make a decision? If not, who had the authority to push the button?"*[1] As the law now stands, the answer is—*no one:*

> The President stands alone as the supreme authority of the Executive branch of government. The Cabinet and National Security Council can advise him but cannot act for him. They cannot become a collective commander-in-chief of the armed forces, or sign legislation into law, or appoint judges, or decide high policies of government. . . . Constitutionally, the Vice President is designated by the voters to take over only "in case of the removal of the President from office, or of his death, resignation or inability to discharge the powers and duties of said office. . . ." The Constitution does not make clear what it means by "inability to discharge the powers and duties of said office." It does not say who shall decide when a President is disabled, whether the Vice President assumes the "powers and duties" of the presidency or the "office" itself, and just how a President who recovers his health can recover his office. . . .*[2]

---

his secret operation for cancer of the jaw; or the two hours and fifteen minutes that Franklin D. Roosevelt was comatose before his death; or the two hours and five minutes that Dwight D. Eisenhower was under anesthesia during an operation for intestinal blockage; or the period of Eisenhower's incapacity following his stroke.

*No clear distinction has been made between the terms *inability* and *disability,* and they appear to be used interchangeably by most of the authorities who have written about presidential succession. In this study unless otherwise specified both *inability* and *disability* refer to any factor or situation, whatever its cause or duration, which renders a President unable to exercise his powers at a time when there is any

Since there is literally no one who can take the President's place, his serious illness can mean—and historically has meant—paralysis to a greater or lesser degree in every branch of the government. But the past damage resulting from this gap in the Constitution is insignificant compared to its potential for catastrophe in the age of the H-bomb and rocket weaponry. Herbert H. Brownell, Jr., who as Eisenhower's Attorney General attempted in vain to secure legislation which would repair the alarming breach in our laws, has summarized the present situation:

The realization has grown among thoughtful people that our very survival in this age may rest on the capacity of the nation's chief executive to make swift and unquestioned decisions in an emergency. As a result, a major constitutional problem, previously glossed over, has been brought to the fore. The problem is that posed by temporary presidential inability to discharge the powers and duties of the presidency at a time when emergency action is required. It has been emphasized during the Eisenhower administration by the President's three periods of temporary physical incapacity, even though, fortunately, no crisis required presidential action during those periods. Now that the issue is so forcefully upon us, with our future existence possibly depending on the forethought that we exercise in resolving it, failure to take proper steps to answer promptly the constitutional question would be the height of irresponsibility.[3]

That we are today unprotected from the consequences of a lapse in executive power is at least in part a result of the American public's misunderstanding—or even total unawareness—of this admittedly complex problem. At present only specialized studies on presidential inability are in print. It is hoped that this book, addressed to the general reader, will serve to clarify the issues involved for a wider audience than political scientists and students of constitutional law. An informed and aroused electorate is the best possible guarantee that our representatives in Washington

---

public business requiring his personal attention. See the discussion in Ruth Silva, *Presidential Succession* (Ann Arbor: University of Michigan Press, 1951), pp. 88–100; also pp. 83–85.

will enact legislation to insure the continuity of leadership essential for the welfare of our nation and of the entire free world.

The interplay of events, personalities, and partisan politics during the series of emergencies which comprise "the year we had no President" is intricately woven into the fabric of American history, and cannot be adequately understood outside that larger pattern. The next three chapters of this book are, therefore, devoted to a chronological account of the "year"—the historical and legal background of the situation in which we find ourselves today. Chapter V considers the stopgap measures taken by Presidents Eisenhower and Kennedy to provide for delegation of executive powers in the event of temporary presidential inability; Chapter VI reviews pertinent colonial and state legislation; and Chapter VII proposes a basis for action which would permanently resolve the question.

Although the problems of presidential inability have their origin in the Constitutional Convention of 1787, the first of the emergencies which focused attention on the gap in the presidential succession law occurred in 1841, and the following survey opens in that year.

Chapter II

A Violation of Grammar

1. TIPPECANOE AND TYLER, TOO

After fifty years of national existence our country was a lusty and rapidly growing youngster, still a long way from attaining the stature of a world power. We were not much concerned either in or with foreign affairs: the dispute with England over the Oregon border was about our only real problem in the international sphere. Of the twenty-six states in the Union, none lay west of the ninety-fifth parallel, but even though settling the mighty stretch of land beyond the Missouri was still largely unfinished business, migration westward already had begun on a measurable scale.

The population was nearly eighteen million—mostly farmers, many of whom were also pioneers with some record of military service. This combination of factors had led to the political ascendancy of President Andrew Jackson, soldier and pioneer. For a time some of Jackson's popularity seemed to have rubbed off on his hand-picked successor, Martin Van Buren, who followed him into the White House in 1837. But in the spring of that year a depression hit the land: banks closed, credit was tight, there were crop failures in many areas; and the citizenry, needing a scapegoat, turned on Van Buren. "Old Kinderhook," as he was called, was accused of being an aristocrat—a no-account fop who laced himself up in corsets, scented his whiskers with cologne, and loved old silver and good wine more than he did the common man.

Guided by this caricature—which amounted to a blueprint of the type of candidate most unlikely to be the people's choice in 1840—the Whig party bosses came up with a nominee whose public image was the diametric opposite: General William Henry Harrison, a military hero from the West, who had defeated the Indians at the Battle of Tippecanoe. Hoping to win over some opposition votes, the Whigs chose as Harrison's running mate a renegade Democrat, John Tyler of Virginia. But the party was split on a multitude of issues, and despite the widespread dislike of Van Buren, the Whigs might well have lost the election had it not been for the unwitting help of a Democratic editorial writer. His sarcastic suggestion, appearing in a Baltimore paper, that General Harrison "upon condition of his receiving $2,000 and a barrel of cider . . . would no doubt consent to withdraw his pretensions and spend his days in a log cabin on the banks of the Ohio" was political dynamite.[1] Playing up the contrast between the wine-sipping aristocrat in the White House ("Van, Van is a used up man") and the sturdy, red-blooded son of the frontier, the Whigs rolled out the cider barrel, built log-cabin floats, donned coonskin caps, and went into action to the rollicking strains of "Tippecanoe and Tyler, Too."

The Log Cabin and Hard Cider Campaign has been characterized as "an exhibition of abuse, evasion, and irrelevancies on a scale unparalleled in United States history up to that time."[2] But it enabled Harrison and Tyler to carry nineteen of the twenty-six states—and incidentally enriched American political iconography with a flock of still-potent symbols. That Harrison had never lived in a log cabin and detested hard cider is probably quite beside the point.

The sixty-eight-year-old President-elect arrived in Washington on a wet, cold February day. It was raining, with the rain fast turning into snow, but he walked bareheaded up Pennsylvania Avenue to his rooms. There he immediately began to work on his Inaugural Address. Running some eight thousand words, this document is remarkable only for being the longest and, without question, dullest Inaugural Address on record. Its delivery on March 4, 1841, consumed an hour and a half, during which the President stood in the rain, without a hat or topcoat.

The country was still deep in the financial slump, and the people had been anxiously awaiting a statement of the new administration's policies. Harrison's mammoth oration did little to reassure or enlighten them. His only memorable campaign utterance had been the promise that if elected he would never use the veto and would strive to diminish the influence of the executive branch. In his Inaugural Address he harped on this theme ("it is preposterous to suppose . . . the President, placed at the capital, in the center of the country could better understand the wishes of the people than their own immediate representatives who spend a part of every year among them . . ."),[3] outlining a program which would leave the initiative in government to the Congress and, more specifically, to his friend Henry Clay, then senator from Kentucky.

It may be conjectured that one of the more restive listeners—at least, inwardly—was the new Vice President, John Tyler. He had quite different views from Harrison on the role of the Chief Executive in government; if it had been left up to him, there would have been no talk of surrendering the presidential prerogatives to the legislative branch. But in 1841 very little *was* left up to the Vice President. The office was regarded as "a comfortable sinecure with which to honor some of the country's more able politicians."[4] On state occasions such as this one a good Vice President was seen and not heard.

The one immediate result of the President's speech was that he came down with a chest cold. Combined with an already existing digestive weakness, probably duodenal ulcers, the cold weakened the old soldier. But he refused to favor himself—was he not, after all, a hardy son of the frontier?—and would not allow any curtailment of his crowded schedule of appointments.

During his first days as President he was pestered by swarms of party workers clamoring for federal appointments. Although it was Andrew Jackson who first applied on a national scale the maxim "To the victors belong the spoils," the Whigs evidently felt that what had been good enough for Old Hickory would be good enough for Old Tippecanoe. At all hours of the day office seekers thronged the White House, hounding the President until he was bone-weary and sick.

One morning they jammed all the lower floor of the White House. Harrison, coming back from a before-breakfast walk with the District marshal, found himself surrounded by a clamoring mob. He appealed to them to leave their recommendations and letters with his secretary. . . . The marshal tried vainly to clear the stairway to the second floor so the aged President could go to his rooms. But the crowd refused to budge until the Chief Executive agreed to take all the letters and recommendations with him personally. With his pockets bulging, and his arms heavily laden, the weary President mounted the stairs.[5]

All during March, Harrison continued his early-morning walks. They often took him to the downtown Washington stores, where he indulged his domestic side by buying all the White House supplies, including the groceries. In the late evenings, though exhausted by the demands of his daily schedule, he paid visits to the various governmental departments.

One morning on his way to market—as usual, wearing neither cloak nor topcoat—the President was drenched by a heavy rain. His wet clothes gave him a chill, the chill aggravated his cold, the cold developed into pneumonia, and exactly one month after taking office President William Henry Harrison was dead.

The President's illness had first been diagnosed as pneumonia in the lower right lobe of his lung, complicated by congestion of the liver. Suction cups and stinging ointments were applied to his right side, the doctors apparently theorizing that this would draw the infection out through the skin. They also dosed him with laxatives—calomel and castor oil, rhubarb and emetic ipecac—and the resultant vomiting and diarrhea soon dissipated the patient's remaining strength. When his physicians finally realized that their "treatments" had brought the President to the threshold of death, they administered such antidotes as opium, camphor, and brandy. But it was too late: ". . . profuse diarrhea came on, under which he sank at thirty minutes to one o'clock on the morning of the fourth. . . ." The President's last words, obviously addressed to posterity, were as high-flown and as innocuous as his Inaugural Address: "Sir, I wish you to understand the true principles of Government. I wish them carried out. I ask nothing more."[6]

All the members of the Cabinet had been present when the President passed away; Vice President Tyler, however, was at his home in Williamsburg, Virginia. That same night an official message notifying him of the President's death was composed and signed by the Cabinet members, and entrusted to Fletcher Webster, the son and assistant of Secretary of State Daniel Webster.[7] He was on his way before dawn via stagecoach and chartered boat. The boat took him as far as Yorktown; there he transferred to horseback and galloped hell-for-leather the last ten miles to Williamsburg.

His arrival put an end to a happy, boisterous family scene: the Vice President was hunkered down on a gravel walk, shooting marbles with his two sons. In high good humor, he was heckling the youngsters, who were losing to him. That marble game was probably the last time John Tyler enjoyed himself for four years.

There was a few hours' delay while Tyler, who was short of funds, arranged to borrow several hundred dollars; then the two men started back to Washington on the government-chartered boat. While young Webster slept, the Vice President paced the deck in solitude. He was confronted with one of the most momentous decisions in American history, and he was called upon to make it under circumstances in which neither he nor any other man could be expected to maintain an objective point of view.

The situation was without precedent. Never before had a Chief Executive died in office. The country had, in effect, been without a President for two days. What happened next depended on the construction Tyler put on Article II, Section 1, Clause 5 of the Constitution—the clause which deals with the succession in the event of presidential inability.* The relevant passage reads as follows:

*There has been inconsistency in citing this provision of the Constitution. Some authorities refer to the passage as Clause 6, instead of Clause 5, as it is designated in this book; others use "Paragraph" in place of "Clause." The irregularity may be ascribed to the fact that in the original document the part under number "2" of Article II, Section 1 contained two paragraphs, the second of which was superseded by the Twelfth Amendment. Regardless of the method of reference used in the sources the intention in every instance is unmistakable.

In Case of the Removal of the President from Office, or of his Death, Resignation, or Inability to discharge the Powers and Duties of the said Office, the Same shall devolve on the Vice President. . . .

At first glance this may seem clear enough, but there is an ambiguity in the wording. Does "the Same" refer to the "Powers and Duties" of the presidency, or to "the said Office" itself?

If Tyler interpreted "the Same" as referring to "Powers and Duties," he would remain the Vice President exercising the powers and duties of the dead President. If he decided that "the Same" referred to "the said Office," he would become the tenth President of the United States.

On his arrival in Washington, Tyler was met at the dock by the Cabinet and escorted to Brown's Indian Queen Hotel on Pennsylvania Avenue. A note was sent to Judge William Cranch, Chief Justice of the Circuit Court of the District of Columbia, summoning him to the hotel. Cranch was taken to Tyler's rooms, where in the presence of the Cabinet, of Fletcher Webster, the tavernkeeper Jesse Brown, and some hotel guests, he administered the Presidential Oath of Office.

Directly after the ceremony the seventy-two-year-old jurist signed the following affidavit:

I, William Cranch, . . . certify that the above-named John Tyler personally appeared before me this day, and although he deems himself qualified to exercise the powers and office of President on the death of William Henry Harrison, late President of the United States, without any other oath than that which he has taken as Vice President, yet as doubts may arise, and for greater caution, took and subscribed the foregoing [Presidential] oath before me.[8]

Who decided that Tyler should become President instead of Acting President? Was it his decision alone or reached in consort with the Cabinet? When was the decision made? These are questions to which we may never have a clear answer. All that can be stated with certainty is that the Cabinet publicly announced the President's death, sent a notification addressed to "John Tyler, Vice President of the United States,"[9] and was present when he was sworn in on April 6, 1841. None of the published papers of Tyler or of the five Cabinet members present— Secretary of State Daniel Webster, Secretary of the Treasury Thomas Ewing, Secretary of War John Bell, Attorney General John J. Crittenden, Postmaster General Francis Granger—sheds any light on the matter.*

There are three schools of thought: (1) Tyler himself decided he would have presidential status, promptly claimed it, and was unopposed by the Cabinet; (2) Daniel Webster thought that Tyler's action violated the Constitution, but did not make an issue of it because they belonged to the same political party; and (3) Webster, far from opposing Tyler's assumption of office, was the one who decided that he should become President. According to this third version, only Webster among those in official circles thought that President Harrison would die, or at best would be disabled for a long period; he discussed these contingencies with the Cabinet, giving it as his opinion that in either event Tyler would be President, and urged that he be sent for. But no record of such a discussion can be found. After Harrison's death, Webster had the Clerk of the Supreme Court write to Chief Justice Roger B. Taney, who was in Maryland, asking him to come and confer on the question of whether or not Tyler should take the Presidential Oath. Taney refused to do so without a formal invitation from the Cabinet or from the Vice President, and further explained that he didn't want to appear to be intruding in the business of a coordinate branch of the government.[10]

Who, then, did decide that Tyler should take the oath of office? On the face of it, the affidavit signed by Judge Cranch would seem to indicate that Tyler thought the oath was unnecessary—that he believed the office of President automatically devolved on him when Harrison died.[11] On the other hand, if he thought that he had become "no more than Acting President, the oath he had previously taken to discharge the duties of the Vice President would cover the whole ground, as one of the prescribed duties of that office

---

*The sixth member of the Cabinet, Secretary of the Navy George Ticknor Curtis, was absent from Washington at this time.

. . . is that of acting as President in the event of the President's death."[12] There is still a third possibility: if Tyler was uncertain of his status—if he was not sure that he automatically succeeded to the Presidency—but wished to lay claim to the office

it would appear from a plain reading of the Constitution that he was legally enjoined to subscribe to the oath provided especially for the President. For Article Two, Section One, provides that: *"Before he enter on the Execution of his Office, he shall take the following Oath or Affirmation. . . ."* The act of taking the oath marks the President's first official act in office. The doubts that might arise, then, would have been well founded, as Cranch said, if Tyler laid claim to the presidential office without ever taking the presidential oath. The "greater caution" appears to have been the mark both of prudence and of necessity.[13]

In short, all that can be said without fear of successful contradiction is that Tyler *or somebody* decided he should be President; Tyler *or somebody* decided he should take the oath of office; Tyler *or somebody* decided he should put it on the record that he did not believe the oath was necessary. However, since the Cabinet was present when he took the oath and since no evidence to the contrary exists, it *can* be asserted with some confidence that Webster and the other Cabinet members did not regard Tyler as a usurper.

Newspaper opinion was divided. Those holding that Tyler's decision (as it will be referred to for convenience) was right included the *Boston Courier* (Whig), the *Washington Globe* and the *Pennsylvanian* (both Democratic), the *Raleigh Register* (Whig), and the principal Whig paper, the *National Intelligencer* (Philadelphia and Washington). Among those holding that Tyler should remain Vice President or Acting President were two other Boston papers (one Whig, one Democratic), the *New York Post* (Democratic), a Harrisburg paper (Whig), and the *Richmond Enquirer* (Democratic). None of the major newspapers suggested that a special election be called.[14]

Other dissident parties included an elder statesman, former President John Quincy Adams, and not unexpectedly, Henry Clay. On April 9, 1841, Tyler made an Inaugural Address, and on April 14 he moved into the White House. Two days later Adams wrote in his diary:

I paid a visit this morning to Mr. Tyler, who styles himself President . . . and not Vice-President acting as President. . . . But it is a construction in direct violation of both the grammar and context of the Constitution . . . a strict constructionist would warrant more than a doubt whether the Vice-President has the right to occupy the President's house, or to claim his salary, without an Act of Congress.[15]

Clay picked up Adams' argument that Tyler was Acting President only and carried it a step farther, declaring that he did not have all the powers of a regularly chosen Chief Executive,[16] but by the time the matter came up in the Senate (June), 1841), he either had changed his mind or had decided it was no use to fight a *fait accompli*: at any rate, he voted to give Tyler the presidential title. A somewhat longer debate in the House the day before had ended with the defeat of a resolution that Tyler be styled "Acting President." This congressional action appeared to close the succession issue, and by the end of June "even John Quincy Adams referred to Tyler as 'the President.' "[17]

And yet Adams had been right. Tyler's accession to the office of President was contrary to the Constitution.

2. THE CONSTITUTION AND THE TYLER PRECEDENT

Memorable details are sometimes misleading. History has recorded that John Tyler was playing marbles with his two boys when he received word of President Harrison's death. The picture evoked is that of an innocent bystander caught up willy-nilly in the tide of great events—a man upon whom (in the words of a later Vice President who acceded to the Presidency) "a bull or a load of hay" has suddenly fallen.[18] But Tyler was a long way from being an innocent bystander, and there is evidence that he was not unprepared for the news that Fletcher Webster brought him. In a letter dated some six months after he took over

the Presidency, he wrote to his friend and confidant Little-
ton W. Tazewell:

> I well remember your prediction of Gen. Harrison's death,
> and with what emphasis you enquired of me whether I had
> thought of my own situation upon the happening of that
> contingency. You declared in advance much of the difficulty
> by which I have already been surrounded.[19]

It is a good deal more than a reasonable supposition
that Tyler *had* given some thought to his "own situation":
it would be incredible if he had not. A Jeffersonian Democrat and an extreme state rights man, he had little in common with the Whigs except their announced opposition to
the consolidation of power in Washington. During his
thirty years in public office, he had served in both houses
of Congress and as governor of Virginia. The record showed
that he was independent, stubborn, outspoken, and courageous; he knew what he was against but not always what he
was for. Although he had stood with Jackson against a re-
charter of Nicholas Biddle's Bank of the United States,
Tyler felt that when the President removed the government's deposits from the bank he had (in the terms of the
resolution censuring Jackson) "assumed upon himself
authority and power not conferred by the Constitution";
and rather than vote to expunge this censure from the
record, Tyler resigned from the Senate in February, 1836.
Having thus cut himself off from his own party, he allied
himself with the newly formed Whig party, and in 1838 was
again a candidate for the Senate. This ran counter to the
plans of Henry Clay, who was conniving to obtain the
senatorship for William C. Rives. Tyler's friends "demanded
a showdown. At first, Clay pleaded 'not guilty' to the
charge of intrigue. But finally . . . the Kentuckian admitted his activities in behalf of Rives, and offered a compromise: Rives would be elected to the Senate, and Tyler
would be given the Whig vice-presidential nomination in
1840."[20]

Whether or not Clay actually intended to keep his end
of the bargain, when convention time came nothing could
stop the movement for Tyler. As consolation for Clay, there

was the knowledge that Tyler would attract votes of the Southern state rights faction, and that once he was "safely embalmed" in the Vice Presidency, he would present little threat to Clay's legislative program. With President Harrison already committed to a role of passive approval while his friend Harry Clay did the wheeling and dealing, and with four of the six Cabinet members "Clay pigeons," it must have seemed to the crafty, craggy senator from Kentucky that he had the executive branch well under control.

While there is no way of knowing how much thought Tyler gave to the presidential succession clause, the possibility that it might be evoked, as his letter to Tazewell shows, was certainly not unforeseen, and his actions seem to indicate that he was predisposed to take advantage of the opportunity offered him by its ambiguous wording. For one thing, as previously noted, the official message which interrupted his marble game was addressed to "John Tyler, Vice-President of the United States"—an indication that the Cabinet members did not consider he had automatically succeeded to the Presidency on Harrison's death. Nevertheless, and with a minimum of delay, Tyler put himself on record to the contrary—he deemed himself qualified to exercise the powers and office of President "without any other oath than that which he has taken as Vice-President, [but] as doubts may arise and for greater caution" consolidated his position by taking the Presidential Oath. Moreover, his "whole course of conduct in the first few days after he arrived in the capital demonstrated plainly that he acted with conscious deliberation to establish himself as President in his own right and not as a mere caretaker for the departed Harrison."[21]

Whether or not his decision had been weighed in advance of the contingency or was only reached after discussion with the Cabinet, it certainly appears, as one writer put it, that Tyler did not enter into any abstract reasoning about the Constitution.[22] The wording of the succession clause gave him an opening, and he took it. But assuming that he had been determined to be guided by the intent of the framers of the Constitution, what might he have done to ascertain it?

For one thing, he might have studied the records of the Constitutional Convention of 1787: Madison's *Notes* had been published in 1840. However, there is no evidence that Tyler referred to them or that he even knew of their existence.[23] As a lawyer he would be aware that precedents would, at least to some degree, affect the thinking of the delegates, but locating historical materials on the inability provisions of colonial and state charters would have required months of research, for records were scattered and libraries few. And he could not consult any of the men who had drafted the Constitution; the youngest of the signers, James Madison, had died six years before. Of course, old John Quincy Adams was still alive. He had been twenty when the Constitutional Convention was held, and although he had not signed the Constitution, as the son of the second President and himself a former President, he must have heard the matter discussed. But Adams, though a fellow Whig, had little use for Tyler—and Tyler knew it. Adams' opinion of him is summed up in diary entry made on the day of Harrison's death:

Tyler is a political sectarian of the slave-driving, Virginian, Jeffersonian school, principled against all improvement, with all the interests and passions and vices of slavery rooted in his moral and political constitution—with talents not above mediocrity, and a spirit incapable of expansion to the dimensions of the station upon which he has been cast by the hand of Providence. . . . This day was in every sense gloomy.[24]

Ironically enough, the one man who might have told Tyler the intent of the framers of the Constitution was about the last man he would have wished to consult.

The historical materials bearing on the presidential succession clause were first put into focus by a brilliant Washington lawyer, Henry E. Davis, in a monograph, *Inability of the President,* written in the summer of 1881 while President Garfield lay ill in the White House.* It remained unprinted until 1918, at which time it appeared in the *Congressional Record.*[25] Davis' monograph offers proof, never rebutted, that the Vice President was never intended to be more than Acting President. In summary, this is what Davis found:

The Constitutional Convention of 1789 was organized in the same manner as conventions held today, with most of the work parceled out to committees. Davis discovered that two resolutions regarding presidential inability (or disability: both words were used) were presented to the Convention as a whole. *Both* resolutions provided that the Vice President would act as President during the disability of the Chief Executive. *Both* resolutions gave only the right to exercise the powers and duties of the office to the Acting President.

The general idea was approved by the entire Convention, and the two resolutions were referred to a five-man committee "to revise the style and arrange the article agreed to by the House."[26] The sole function of this committee was to combine the resolutions, polish their language, and fit them harmoniously into the body of the Constitution. It had no power to alter or amend any of the sections sent to it. But in combining and condensing, the committee changed the intended sense, as a comparison of the two texts makes clear.

Articles Originally Agreed to by the Convention	*After Consolidation by the Committee on Style and Later Adopted*
Article X, Section 2: . . . and in case of his removal as aforesaid, death, absence, resignation or inability to discharge the powers or duties of his office, the Vice President shall exercise those powers and duties until another President be chosen, or until the inability of the President be removed.	Article II, Section 1, Clause 5: In case of the removal of the president from office, or of his death, resignation, or inability to discharge the powers and duties of the said office, the same shall devolve on the vice-president,
Article X, Section 1: The Legislature may declare by law what officer of the United States shall act as President, in case of the death, resignation, or disability of the President and Vice President;	and the Congress may by law provide for the case of removal, death, resignation or inability, both of the president and vice-president, declaring what officer shall then act as president,

*The unabridged text of the monograph is given in Appendix I.

and such Officer shall act accordingly, until such disability be removed, or a President shall be elected.	and such officer shall act accordingly, until the disability be removed, or a president shall be elected.

Attorney General Robert F. Kennedy has analyzed the changes as follows:

When we refer to the provisions before and after the Committee on Style had combined them, it appears that the Committee did several things: consolidated two provisions into one and introduced the words "the same shall devolve on the Vice President"; omitted reference to "absence" as an occasion for operation of the succession rule; used the adverbial clause "until the disability be removed," only once instead of using it to modify each of the preceding clauses separately; substituted "inability" for "disability" in the clause referring to succession beyond the Vice President, possibly as being more comprehensive and covering both absence and temporary disability; and changed the semicolon after "Vice President" to a comma so that the limited beginning, "and such Officer" clause would refer to both the Vice President and officer designated by Congress. Thus the evolution of this clause makes clear that merely the powers and duties devolve on the Vice President, not the office itself.[27]

The proceedings of the Federal Convention offer further proof that the delegates never intended the Vice President to become President during a temporary or permanent inability of the President. James Wilson, Gouverneur Morris, and James Madison objected strongly to a proposal for election of the President by Congress because they feared the Congress would purposely delay in filling any vacancy in order that its own presiding officer could act as President during the interim.[28] Charles Warren, in *The Making of the Constitution*, stresses the delegates' repeated reference to the idea that "the Vice President would only perform the duties of President until a new election for President should be held; and that he would not ipso facto become President."[29] This interpretation was carried over into the ratifying conventions of the states, at which the delegates spoke of the "Vice President, when acting as President."[30]

Attorney General Robert F. Kennedy has presented an irrefutable argument in support of this general thesis by looking at the Constitution in its entirety. If the Tyler interpretation is applied to both temporary and permanent inability, certain other sections become inconsistent. For example:

1. Article I, Section 3, Clause 5 says the Senate shall choose a President pro tempore in the absence of the Vice President or "when he shall exercise the Office of President of the United States."

2. The twelfth amendment provides that if, in case of a contested presidential election, the House of Representatives shall not choose a President before Inauguration Day, "then the Vice President shall act as President in the case of the death or other constitutional disability of the President."[31] This wording assumes even greater importance when it is recalled that the twelfth amendment was adopted on September 25, 1804.

3. Section 3 of the twentieth amendment recognizes the distinction between permanent and temporary inability by providing that if, at the time fixed for beginning the term of the President, the President-elect has died, then the Vice President "shall become President." But the amendment further provides that if a President has not been chosen by the time fixed for the beginning of his term, or if the President-elect fails to qualify, then the Vice President-elect shall "act as President until the President qualifies. . . ."[32]

The records and history of the Constitutional Convention and consideration of other provisions in the Constitution establish indisputably that it was the intention of the framers for the Vice President to be *Acting President* in the event of presidential inability. He was *not* to succeed to the Presidency on the death of the President; he could become President *only* by being elected to the office. As Edward S. Corwin puts it,

That Tyler was wrong in his reading of the original intention of the Constitution is certain.* It was clearly the

---

*"One may logically ask why doubt and controversy over the meaning of this clause has arisen in the past, if the framers' intent is so clear and certain. The answer is simply that a great deal more is now known

expectation of the Framers that the Vice-President remain Vice-President, a stopgap, a locum tenens, whatever the occasion of his succession. . . .[33]

The misinterpretation of the Constitution in 1841, in the words of John Quincy Adams, placed "in the Executive chair a man never thought of for it by anybody."[34] During the next twenty-five years two Presidents died in office—Zachary Taylor on July 9, 1850, and Abraham Lincoln on April 14, 1865. On both occasions the precedent set by Tyler was followed and on both occasions John Quincy Adams' remark applied: Vice Presidents Millard Fillmore and Andrew Johnson took the oath of office and became, respectively, the thirteenth and seventeenth Presidents of the United States. Thus, in the twenty-eight-year period between the inauguration of President Harrison in 1841 and the inaguration of President Ulysses S. Grant in 1869, during more than a third of that time—ten years and five months—presidential powers were exercised by men who had received no popular mandate to do so.

However, "the more pernicious consequences of the precedent . . . do not manifest themselves in cases of vacancy, but appear in cases of inability."[35] The nature of these consequences first became apparent in 1881 when the Tyler precedent, which previously had been followed in cases of the death of the President in office, was applied to a basically different situation—that of prolonged presidential inability.

---

about what went on at the Constitutional Convention of 1787 than was known in the past, even in the years immediately after the Convention. It was conducted in secrecy, and not until Madison's notes were published posthumously in 1840 was a fair picture available, although still not a complete one. Farrand's work, *Records of the Federal Convention of 1787*, the definitive source on the subject, did not appear until 1911. Other important data have come to light subsequently through the research of biographers and historians dealing with persons and actions of the time. Understandably, it has taken years for scholars to bring the information together. Furthermore, confusing precedents have been established by officials who did not have access to this information" (Brownell, "Presidential Disability," pp. 192–193).

Chapter III

Practical Politics

Practical politics consists in ignoring the facts.
—The Education of Henry Adams

1. THE GARFIELD INTERREGNUM

Unparalleled prosperity in the South and West—a national surplus of $145,000,000—a *reduction* in postal rates: the jubilant tone of such headlines as these reflect the state of the nation at the opening of the 1880's. Railroad construction had expedited the settling of the Trans-Missouri West; telegraphic communications united the remote sections of the country; and the Atlantic cable linked us to the Old World. There were thirty-eight states in the Union now, and the population had risen to fifty million. Cities were growing in size and influence. Farming was still the leading occupation, but the tide was shifting from country to city as factories and offices drew into their orbit not only immigrants but thousands of native-born Americans from small towns and villages.

The 1870's had been a period of federal and municipal corruption, with the big city bosses muscling into control of the Republican party. Graft and grabbing had reached a climax during President Grant's second administration; but reform was under way by the time his successor, Rutherford B. Hayes, took office. At the Republican Convention of 1880, the reform element of the party, the "Halfbreeds," fought it out with the "Stalwarts," the faction of the bosses and spoilsmen. The resulting ticket—James A. Garfield for President; Chester A. Arthur for Vice President—obviously represented a marriage of convenience.

When the convention opened, Garfield, then senator-elect from Ohio, and his fellow Halfbreeds supported James G. Blaine, the senator from Maine and former speaker of the House. Arthur was aligned with the Stalwarts, who were backing former President Grant for a third term.

When Grant and Blaine were deadlocked after twenty-eight ballots, a swing toward Garfield began, climaxed by his nomination on the thirty-sixth ballot. Since Garfield was only forty-nine and in good health, the Halfbreeds saw no risk in appeasing the Stalwarts with the vice presidential nomination. So it came about that Garfield, a Civil War hero and a man of notable integrity, was paired off with "Chet" Arthur, whose name was associated with bossism and machine politics.

Party unity endured only until the election campaign had been won. Signs of a new split appeared when Garfield appointed Blaine his Secretary of State. Blaine's bitterest foe was the Stalwart boss, Senator Roscoe Conkling of New York, and Conkling quarreled violently with the President over the appointment. Unperturbed, Garfield continued with his program for civil service reform, naming a Conkling opponent to be Collector of the Port of New York. This was a patronage-rich job on which the Stalwarts had depended for much of their strength in the state, and Conkling and Platt—the junior New York senator—resigned their offices in protest. They counted on being immediately re-elected,* a demonstration of strength which they figured would serve as a "Keep Off" sign if Garfield and Blaine planned on any future meddling in New York State politics. It was a good idea, but it backfired: New Yorkers had not forgotten the scandals of the Grant administration. When it became apparent that the issue was in doubt, Vice President Arthur—in direct opposition to the President's wishes—came to the support of his old cronies. In spite of his efforts, they were defeated, and now there could be no concealing the hostility between the President and the Vice President.

The defeat of Conkling and Platt on their home grounds, combined with the paralyzing setbacks the President had handed the Stalwarts in Congress, measurably increased Garfield's stature as a politician as well as his reputation for integrity. Seldom had a presidential administration opened more auspiciously; at this juncture, three

*Senators were elected by the state legislature at this time.

months after Garfield's inauguration, a disappointed office seeker belonging to the Stalwart faction, a lawyer named Charles Guiteau, changed the course of history with a bullet.

At 9:20 on the morning of July 2, 1881, the President arrived at the Baltimore & Potomac station en route to commencement exercises at his alma mater, Williams College. He was accompanied by Secretary of State Blaine. Near the door as the President's party came in was Guiteau, armed with an English Bulldog 44-caliber revolver. Garfield and Blaine started walking briskly through the waiting room, and Guiteau rushed after them. Coming up behind the President, he fired twice at his back before the crowd closed in and seized him.

The President cried out, and then slumped to the floor. He was placed on a mattress and carried to an office on the second floor of the station. Within minutes several doctors had gathered. According to the report of Dr. D. W. Bliss, a well-known Washington surgeon who was later placed in charge of the case, they found that the President exhibited all the symptoms of shock and internal hemorrhage. The second bullet had only grazed his right coat sleeve, but the first had entered his back about four inches to the right of the spinal column at the height of the eleventh rib. In an attempt to locate the bullet, the wound was explored with a probe, the probe being turned this way and that to find the channel carved by the bullet. The instrument became stuck in the shattered fragments of the rib, and was only withdrawn with great difficulty. The doctor then inserted his little finger in the wound but still was unable to locate the bullet, and concluded that it had probably entered the liver. At 10:20 A.M. the President was taken by horse-drawn ambulance to the White House.

Although he had not been expected to live through the night, the President was much improved the next day. However, the exploration of the wound had been conducted under far from sterile conditions and, not surprisingly, an infection developed. From July 2, the date of the shooting, to August 10, the President's condition varied: one day he would feel fairly well, the next he would run a high temperature and have difficulty keeping his food down. On August 10 he felt strong enough to sign an extradition paper, the first and last official act he performed during his long illness. On August 18 "a swelling of the right parotid gland [the salivary gland below the ear] was noted, accompanied by restlessness and wandering of the mind. These were ominous signs, indicating that the septic bacteria had broken into the blood stream, producing blood poisoning."[1] As the infection spread, abscesses formed in various parts of his body and he was afflicted with facial paralysis. But he rallied again, and at his insistence was taken to a cottage by the sea at Elberon, New Jersey.

While the President lingered between life and death, only routine business was transacted by the government. The Cabinet had no authority to act on many of the matters that came up, and the President was too ill to be consulted.

Although [Garfield's] mind was clear during the first weeks of his invalidism, the daily bulletins of the physicians are sufficient evidence that he was physically unable to discharge the duties of his office. During these eighty days a great deal of urgent business demanded the President's immediate attention: there were postal frauds; officers did not perform their duties because they had not been commissioned; the country's foreign relations were deteriorating. . . . Nearly every day the newspapers mentioned some important matter which was ignored simply because it required the President's personal attention. At one time there was a rumor that the Central Pacific Railway would bring action for a writ of mandamus directing Vice President Arthur to assume the President's powers and duties during Garfield's illness [*Boston Evening Transcript*, August 25, 1881], but no action was taken. The Cabinet continued to conduct the affairs of government as best it could without an active Chief Executive.[2]

Public opinion, as reflected in the newspapers, indicated that there were some who felt governmental business was being handled satisfactorily, but "New York's two leading papers, the *Times* and the *Herald*, objected editorially to having the affairs of state managed by the Cabinet, a body unknown to the Constitution, [and] particularly disapproved of Secretary of State James G. Blaine's activities—activities which made him a kind of *de facto* President [*New York Times,* August 11, 1881; *New York Herald,* September 5, 1881]."[3]

In the first days of September, the Cabinet called a meeting to consider the possibility of asking Vice President Arthur to act as President. At this time Garfield's condition had taken a turn for the better, and it was believed that he would recover. But in the physicians' opinion at least another two months would elapse before he would be back at his desk, and already his long illness had paralyzed the transaction of government business in every executive department. It was essential that the Cabinet take steps to relieve the situation.

Except for Secretary of State Blaine and the young Secretary of War, Robert T. Lincoln (who was the lone Stalwart present at the meeting), the names of the Cabinet members are forgotten by all save historians. But with the President incapacitated, these men were, in effect, "running the country," and a brief consideration of the composition of the Garfield Cabinet may provide some insight into their qualifications to do so.

The Garfield administration, so far as its Cabinet was concerned, was completed during the last twenty-four hours preceding the inauguration. There was great difficulty in filling the post of Secretary of the Treasury. . . . [The President] made the first offer to Senator Allison of Iowa. He . . . finally declined, preferring to stay in the Senate. . . . Senator Windom, whose term was about to expire, was offered the place, and he accepted the night before inauguration. He had been associated with Mr. Garfield in the Senate, was in the confidence of Mr. Blaine, and was very intimate with the latter in the Senate. . . . The entire Cabinet was made up in accordance with the wishes of Mr. Blaine; not a single element antagonistic to him was admitted. . . .

Mr. Windom in the Treasury gave satisfaction as a good business administrator. He was a safe, careful man, but he was not original. He would have been incapable of outlining any determined or bold policy, but he was very faithful and discreet in carrying out the orders of a superior mind.

In the War Department, Mr. Lincoln, then a young lawyer without the slightest experience in public affairs, began to learn his duties. In the Navy Department was W. H. Hunt, a former Judge of the Court of Claims. He was a well-equipped lawyer with a good knowledge of affairs, but he was comparatively unknown to the public, and represented no active element in political life, although he was put in as the representative of the South. In the Interior Department was Mr. Kirkwood, a former Senator. He was an amiable old gentleman, very slow and lethargic in his movements, possessing strong common sense and good abilities, but having none of the executive qualities of an administrator necessary for a great department. . . . The Attorney General was Wayne MacVeigh, of Pennsylvania, a corporation lawyer without any previous public experience. He owed his election to the fact that he was a son-in-law of Simon Cameron. He made no record for himself during the brief period of his career, except as a disorganizing element. . . . The Post-office Department was given to Thomas L. James of New York City, another gentleman wholly unknown to public life, and whose experience had been entirely in commercial affairs.[4]

The account concludes with the observation that except for Blaine the Cabinet was generally considered a weak one, and it was said that the Secretary of State "had the administration so completely under his will that the President was virtually his private secretary and the Cabinet a board of recording scribes."

Three reasons are generally assigned for Arthur's not being asked to take over the powers and duties of the President. First, there was Arthur's political position: he belonged to the wrong wing of the party; he had campaigned for Blaine's dearest enemy; he was identified with "Boss" Conkling and the scandals of the Grant administration. In the Cabinet's view, if Arthur once took over executive power the President's civil service reform program would be washed down the drain in a flood of patronage. (As later events proved, Arthur was neither a "tool of the bosses" nor a saboteur of reform; when he finally did become President he showed himself to be an able and courageous administrator.) The other two reasons referred to the presidential inability clause. There was no agreement either on what inability meant or how it should be established; and it was not certain that if the powers and duties of the President devolved upon Arthur that they could be returned to Garfield when he recovered.

Leading journals and periodicals queried outstanding legal figures on the constitutional problems involved.

The answers to the questions were conflicting and confusing. Many thought that mental inability was the only one covered by the Constitution. . . . Other equally competent legal authorities thought the word "inability" covered any case in which a duty should be discharged but which the President was unable to perform, whatever the reason. A number of lawyers and legislators held that disability must be permanent and must extend throughout the entire term in order to be "inability" in the constitutional sense. . . .

One cause for inaction was that no one knew exactly how the existence of inability should be established. Legal opinion on this question was just as conflicting as opinion on the meaning of "inability." Although some thought that the courts, the Congress, or the Cabinet should decide that the President was disabled, or even that the irrational President [Garfield was then having hallucinations] should do so, most informed opinion supported the position that the Vice President should determine that the President was incapacitated. . . .

Would Vice President Arthur become President for the remainder of the term if called to act as such during the period of Garfield's recuperation? Some respected lawyers and jurists held that he would succeed to the presidential office just as in the case of vacancy, and that, once the powers and duties devolved upon him, they could not be returned to the President when he recovered. Although most lawyers thought that the President would resume his powers and duties when he regained his health, the Cabinet was impressed by arguments to the contrary.[5]

Newspapers on September 2, 1881, carried the story that in the opinion of a majority of the Cabinet assigning the exercise of presidential power to Arthur would amount to ousting Garfield; and that they should not propose Arthur's succession without first letting the President know of this possible consequence. But the President, they felt, was too ill for such a matter to be brought before him; and if they went ahead, they feared the shock might be fatal. Action was postponed.

The President's death on September 19 resolved the stalemate. During the last days of his illness, his disability was mental as well as physical: on September 16 even the *Boston Evening Transcript,* "which resisted any suggestion that Arthur might act for Garfield," admitted that he was having hallucinations. An autopsy showed that the doctors in their several attempts to locate the bullet had succeeded only in opening new cavities in the President's back and abdomen, helping along the spread of the infection.

A wire from the Cabinet informed Vice President Arthur of the President's death and advised him "to take the oath of office as President of the United States without delay."[6] The oath was administered by a New York State judge early in the morning of September 20, 1881, in New York; and the ceremony was repeated in Washington the next day, this time by the Chief Justice, so that it would appear in the records of the Supreme Court. Then, at last, Arthur was free to start clearing away the log jam resulting from eighty days without a President.

In four successive State of the Union messages, President Arthur urged the Congress to consider the "intendment of the Constitution" in regard to presidential inability questions—"questions which concern the very existence of the Government and the liberties of the people. . . ."[7] After that, nobody bothered Congress with the matter again for thirty-five years.

The next interregnum was of relatively brief duration beginning on September 6, 1901, when President William McKinley was shot by the anarchist Leon Czolgosz, and ending on September 14 with McKinley's death and the accession of the Vice President, Theodore Roosevelt. But it was followed by the most protracted instance of presidential disability which has yet occurred in our history: the tragic illness of President Woodrow Wilson, with its incalculable consequences not only for our country but for nations all over the globe.

2. THE "MRS. WILSON REGENCY"

A conflict between a President and a Vice President can have its amusing aspects—until the President falls ill. The breach between Woodrow Wilson and Thomas Riley Marshall was unlike that between Garfield and Arthur in that no overt or active hostility was involved. Marshall always felt kindly toward the President, although he didn't like some of his policies; Wilson superficially reciprocated Marshall's good will, but thought him "a small caliber man," more of a court jester than a potential successor.

The few accounts concerning the choice of Marshall as Wilson's running mate in 1912 have one point in common: they all agree that Marshall was second choice, the first being Oscar W. Underwood of Alabama, who declined. Albert S. Burleson, one of Wilson's managers, relates that after Wilson's nomination, he called him at his summer home in Seagirt, New Jersey, to report that the convention was "leaning toward Marshall" for the Vice Presidency. "But he is a very small-caliber man," Wilson said. According to William G. McAdoo, later Wilson's son-in-law as well as his Secretary of the Treasury, it was *he* who suggested Marshall to Wilson, and Wilson said that Marshall would "be acceptable." However, a third version—that of William F. McCombs, Wilson's floor manager at the convention—is given as the correct one in a recent authoritative study of the Vice Presidency.[8] According to this account, McCombs telephoned Wilson that the three top candidates were Governor Burke of North Dakota, Mayor Preston of Baltimore, and Governor Marshall of Indiana. Wilson left it up to McCombs, who decided on Marshall. McCombs then convened eleven leading Wilson supporters, including Burleson, McAdoo, and A. Mitchell Palmer, the future Attorney General. Palmer's name was mentioned for the office, but he was a Pennsylvanian and McCombs objected that he would not draw needed votes from the Middle West and the Far West. When he realized that the group would back Palmer anyway, McCombs quickly announced that it wouldn't be fitting for a mere eleven men to choose the Vice President. He took the battle to the convention floor and Marshall was unanimously nominated.

All three accounts make it clear that the selection of Marshall was not welcomed with much enthusiasm by Wilson. But the Vice Presidency was the price of Marshall's support,[9] and Wilson's remarks while in office show that he regarded Marshall as a necessary evil, harmless if humored.

When Wilson was up for his second term in 1916, a "Dump Marshall" movement got under way. McAdoo and Henry Morgenthau felt that the Vice President had not made the most of his opportunities as Presiding Officer of the Senate: in their opinion he should have used his power to force passage of the administration's program. But Marshall was an experienced and skilful politician. Although his omission of whip-cracking tactics in the Senate may have displeased the more partisan Democrats, he nonetheless had managed to maneuver the President into a position that would have made it extremely embarrassing to drop him from the ticket. "The pleasure of being associated with you," Wilson wrote Marshall at the end of the 1914 session, "grows as the months pass." And the "Dump Marshall" movement notwithstanding, Wilson's pleasure was to have a chance to grow some more. In the 1916 election Indiana was a key state, and this insured Marshall's renomination.

When John Tyler made his decision to take over the Presidency, the dispute with England over the Oregon border dominated our foreign policy. By the time Woodrow Wilson had completed half of his second term in office, he, as President of the United States, had played a major role in determining the boundaries of nearly every European nation. America was not only a world power but a world leader. The forty-eight states had a population of more than a hundred million; overseas we had become the guardians of Filipinos, Samoans, Hawaiians, Nicaraguans, and Cubans. The increase in presidential responsibility from Tyler's time to Wilson's can be suggested, though very inadequately, by comparing the office space used by each. Two or three rooms on the second floor of the White House sufficed for Tyler;

Wilson's executive offices occupied the entire West Wing, which had been constructed during Theodore Roosevelt's administration.

The natural corollary of increased responsibility was increased strain on the incumbent. Wilson's health was good during his first term: he paced himself well, having his meals on time, taking short naps, and getting close to eight hours of sleep at night. After the outbreak of the First World War in August, 1914, the President gradually altered his daily routine to allow more time on the job. As the pressure mounted he became increasingly irritable, and by December, 1918, when he sailed to Europe to attend the peace conference, he was suffering from a recurrence of the nervous stomach that had troubled him in law school.

In Europe the American President was treated like a Messiah—his pathway from the English Channel to Charing Cross was strewn with roses; in Italy candles were lighted in front of his picture. He carried this burden of adoration, this awareness that millions of people looked on him as their champion, to the "Big Four" conference table, where he was subjected to the wily diplomatic in-fighting and rabbit punches of Clemenceau, Lloyd George, and Orlando, practical men who had little use for the starry-eyed idealism of the man from the New World.

It was at the Paris Conference that the terrible pressures and responsibilities overwhelmed the President. He collapsed completely, and was confined to his bed with what was described as a severe case of influenza. That the strain had told in other, more disturbing, ways was evident to members of his entourage.

Even while lying in bed he manifested peculiarities, one of which was to limit the use of all the automobiles to strictly official purposes, when previously he had been so liberal in his suggestions that his immediate party should have the benefit of this possible diversion, in view of the long hours we were working. When he got back on the job, his peculiar ideas were even more pronounced. He now became more obsessed with the idea that every French employee about the place was a spy for the French Government. Nothing we could say would disabuse his mind of this thought. He insisted they all understood English, when, as a matter of fact, there was just one of them among the two dozen or more who understood a single word of English. About this time he also acquired the peculiar notion that he was personally responsible for all the property in the furnished palace he was occupying. He raised quite a fuss on two occasions when he noticed articles of furniture had been removed. Upon investigation—for no one else noticed the change—it was learned that the custodian of the property for the French owner had seen fit to do a little re-arranging. Coming from the President, whom we all knew so well, these were very funny things, and we could but surmise that something queer was happening in his mind.[10]

Americans are often shocked at the idea that some of our Presidents have exhibited the neurotic symptoms we associate with unstable personality, or have suffered so-called nervous breakdowns. John Adams, for example, had such a suspicious disposition that it would be diagnosed as a persecution complex if he lived today. There is no doubt that his inordinate distrust of people affected his judgment at times, particularly in connection with this country's relations with England. Abraham Lincoln was in such an acute depressive state after the death of Ann Rutledge that his friends stayed constantly by his side lest he take his own life. Later on, during his term of office, tension manifested itself in migraine headaches of such severity that his eyeball on the affected side would turn back into his head. In short, we need to remember that our President, whoever he may be, is a human being, and that the office does not carry with it immunity from the ills, physical and mental, to which mortals are subject.

President Wilson was still recuperating from the effects of his illness in Paris when he returned home in July, 1919, to face Senate opposition to American participation in the League of Nations. Wilson was in no condition to do battle, but he decided to make a trip out West to arouse public sentiment in support of the League. According to Joseph P. Tumulty, the President's private secretary:

Admiral Grayson, the President's physician and consistent friend, who knew his condition and the various physical crises through which he had passed here and on the other side, from some of which he had not yet recovered, stood firm in his resolve that the President should not go West, even intimating to me that the President's life might pay the forfeit if his advice were disregarded. Indeed, it needed not the trained eye of a physician to see that the man whom the senators were now advising to make a "swing around the circle" was on the verge of a nervous breakdown. More than once since his return from the Peace Conference I had urged him to take needed rest; to get away from the turmoil of Washington and recuperate; but he spurned this advice and resolved to go through to the end.[11]

After a speech at Pueblo, Colorado, on September 25, 1919, the President again collapsed and was brought back to Washington. The nature of his illness has been characterized variously as a "nervous collapse" and a "stroke."[12] We have it on the authority of former President Herbert Hoover that some of the facts of Wilson's illness were suppressed.[13] At any rate, whatever the cause, the President was incapacitated and was kept in seclusion at the White House.

On October 2, 1919, a cerebral thrombosis partially paralyzed Wilson's left side. Apparently on rising he had gone into the bathroom and was stricken there. Mrs. Wilson dragged him to his bed and called for Dr. Grayson. Ike Hoover, Chief White House Usher, who was in and out of the sickroom several times, has described his condition:

He just lay helpless. True, he had been taking nourishment, but the work the doctors had been doing on him had just about sapped his remaining vitality. All his natural functions had to be artificially assisted and he appeared just as helpless as one could possibly be and live.[14]

For almost a week the President's life hung in the balance. Then he began a slow recovery. When spring came, he was taken for occasional rides in the country, but was so debilitated that, as Ike Hoover notes, he had to sit in the front seat of the car, where he could be propped up. If placed in the back, "he would slide down and topple over as the car rolled along."

As a result of the President's illness our country passed through a period which has been called by some "The Mrs.

Wilson Regency." Why it should be so described will be apparent from the following account written by Edith Bolling Wilson herself:

Once my husband was out of immediate danger, the burning question was how Mr. Wilson might best serve the country, preserve his own life and if possible recover. Many people, among them some I had counted as friends, have written of my overwhelming ambition to act as President; of my exclusion of all advice, and so forth. I am trying here to write as though I had taken the oath to tell the truth, the whole truth, and nothing but the truth—so help me God.

I asked the doctors to be frank with me; that I must know what the outcome would probably be, so as to be honest with the people. They all said that as the brain was as clear as ever, with the progress made in the last few days, there was every reason to think recovery possible. . . . But recovery could not be hoped for, they said, unless the President were released from every disturbing problem during these days of Nature's effort to repair the damage done.

"How can that be," I asked the doctors, "when everything that comes to an Executive is a problem? How can I protect him from problems when the country looks to the President as the leader?"

Dr. Dercum* leaned towards me and said: "Madam, it is a grave situation, but I think you can solve it. Have everything come to you; weigh the importance of each matter, and see if it is possible by consultations with the respective heads of the Departments to solve them without the guidance of your husband. In this way you can save him a great deal. But always keep in mind that every time you take him a new anxiety or problem to excite him, you are turning a knife in an open wound. His nerves are crying out for rest, and any excitement is torture to him."

"Then," I said, "had he better not resign, let Mr. Marshall succeed to the Presidency, and he himself get that complete rest that is so vital to his life?"

"No," the Doctor said, "not if you feel equal to what I

---

*Who's Who for 1910–11 lists Francis Xavier Dercum: "Neurologist to Philadelphia Hospital since 1887; consulting physician Asylum for the Chronic Insane, Wernersville, Pa., since 1893; instructor nervous and mental diseases, Uni. of Pa., 1883–92; Editor, Textbook on Nervous Diseases by various authors" (Author's note).

suggested. For Mr. Wilson to resign would have a bad effect on the country, and a serious effect on our patient. He has staked his life and made his promise to the world to do all in his power to get the Treaty ratified and make the League of Nations complete. If he resigns, the greatest incentive to recovery is gone; and as his mind is clear as crystal he can still do more with even a maimed body than any one else. He has the utmost confidence in you. Dr. Grayson tells me he has always discussed public affairs with you; so you will not come to them uninformed."

So began my stewardship. I studied every paper sent from the different Secretaries or Senators, and tried to digest and present in tabloid form the things that, despite my vigilance, had to go to the President. I, myself, never made a single decision regarding the disposition of public affairs. The only decision that was mine was what was important and what was not, and the *very* important decision of when to present matters to my husband. . . .

These instructions from the medical men were far from easy to carry out. . . . Upon all sides I was literally besieged by those who "must" see the President. But I carried out the directions of the doctors—and my heart was in it. *Woodrow Wilson was first my beloved husband whose life I was trying to save, . . . after that he was the President of the United States.*[15]

Or, to put it less winsomely: *My husband first; what happened to the country was a secondary consideration.*

Wilson's collapse on his Western trip was, of course, widely reported, but there was a complete news blackout after his return to the White House on Sunday, September 28. Vice President Marshall, close to tears, called in person to inquire about the President's condition, but was told nothing. David F. Houston, who served nearly eight years in Wilson's Cabinet as Secretary of Agriculture and briefly, in 1920, as Secretary of the Treasury, wrote that "there was nothing to go on except rumors. There was no direct or authoritative word even to members of Cabinet from the White House or from the physicians. . . . We canvassed the matter among ourselves but none of us could furnish any light."

On Saturday, October 4, Houston saw Wilson's private secretary, Joseph P. Tumulty, at the Shoreham.

He gave me the first direct word I had had concerning the President. He said that the President was paralyzed in one leg and one arm. He expressed grave alarm over the situation. . . .

Sunday I happened to lunch at the Shoreham. I saw the Vice President and Mrs. Marshall sitting at one of the tables. . . . The Vice President was evidently much disturbed and expressed regret that he was being kept in the dark about the President's condition. He asked me if I could give the real facts, which I was unable to do. I could not even repeat what had been told me, because it had been said in confidence. The Vice President expressed the view that he ought to be immediately informed; that it would be a tragedy for him to assume the duties of President, at best; and that it would be equally a tragedy for the people; that he knew many men who knew more about the government than he did; and that it would be especially trying for him if he had to assume the duties without warning. . . .[16]

On Friday, October 3, Secretary of State Robert Lansing called a Cabinet meeting for the following Monday. "The summoning . . . was the outgrowth of an apprehension, in circles very close to the President, that unless there was evidence that the Executive was functioning, Congress might insist upon investigating the President's condition and perhaps upon installing Vice President Marshall in his place. The call for the meeting was issued only after Mr. Lansing had conferred with Secretaries Baker [War] and Lane [Interior]."[17]

According to Houston:

When we met, Lansing said that it was necessary to decide whether or not we should continue to carry on the government—that there was nothing to guide us as to who would decide the question of the ability of the President to discharge the duties of his office.

After the Secretary of State had outlined the situation, someone suggested that, if it was necessary to take the matter up at all, we should do so only after we had secured direct information as to the President's condition and that we should first consult the President's physician. It was decided to ask Doctor Grayson to meet us and to tell us everything he could. While we were waiting we talked informally about the legal situation. There were no pressing matters requiring the President's decision and signature, and, therefore, there was no need for haste. Garfield was incapacitated from July 2d to September 19th, and no action was taken.

Doctor Grayson and Mr. Tumulty soon came into the Cabinet room. Doctor Grayson stated that the President's condition had improved over Sunday, but that he could not say when he would be out of danger—that the scales might tip either way. He added that they might tip the wrong way especially if he was harassed by business matters, and that he should be bothered as little as possible. He told us that he was suffering from a nervous breakdown, from indigestion and a depleted nervous system. . . .

The words "stroke," "apoplexy," or "cerebral hemorrhage" had not been spoken by Dr. Grayson, and he was asked if he could tell the Cabinet more exactly what was the trouble.

He replied that he could add nothing to what he had already said. He added with a sort of twinkle in his eye: "The President asked me what the Cabinet wanted with me and by what authority it was meeting in Washington without a call from him." He said that the President showed no little irritation when he heard that we were holding a Cabinet meeting.

After some further discussion of the matter, the Secretary of State asked Doctor Grayson to tell the President that we met primarily to express our interest in his condition, to get information about him, to extend our sympathy, and to consider such departmental matters as needed attention, as there had been no Cabinet meeting for a month.

This seemed to me an inadequate statement. It looked as if the Secretary of State for some reason had changed his mind as to the purpose of the meeting since the members had begun to gather. If he had called the meeting at a regular time it might have been sufficient and reasonable for him to say that we had held Cabinet meetings at the request of the President during his absence, that we had held no meeting for a month and that, since he was ill, it seemed not inappropriate or in any way at variance with his views that we should meet. Our meeting at the regular time would have been reassuring to the public, properly creating the picture in their mind that the government was going ahead. But the message the Secretary sent was hardly a satisfactory explanation for our meeting at an unusual time.[18]

Lansing's failure to take a stand was not solely because of the Cabinet's obvious reluctance to go into the inability question, or because of Grayson's incomplete and toned-down report. Probably a more important factor was a private conversation between Lansing and Tumulty on the preceding Friday—the day that Lansing had decided to call the Cabinet meeting. There are two versions—Tumulty's and Lansing's—about what passed between them. According to Tumulty:

[Lansing] informed me that he had called diplomatically to suggest that in view of the incapacity of the President, we should arrange to call in the Vice-President to act in his stead as soon as possible. . . .

Lansing then read Article II, Section 1, Clause 5 of the Constitution from a book which he had brought from the State Department, and Tumulty

coldly turned and said: "Mr. Lansing, the Constitution is not a dead letter in the White House. I have read the Constitution and do not find myself in need of any tutoring at your hands on the provision you have just read. . . . You may rest assured that while Woodrow Wilson is lying in the White House on the broad of his back, I will not be a party to ousting him."

At that point, according to Tumulty, Grayson came in and "left no doubt in Mr. Lansing's mind that he would not do as Mr. Lansing suggested." Tumulty added that if anyone outside the White House circle attempted to certify to the President's disability, Grayson and he would "stand together and repudiate it."[19]

Lansing's version is given in Josephus Daniels' *Life of Woodrow Wilson:*

[Tumulty] told me that on Wednesday, October 1, the President had become much worse. I asked him in what way. He did not answer me in words, but significantly put his right hand to his left shoulder and drew it along his left side. Of course, the implication was that the President had suffered a stroke and that his left side was paralyzed.

Lansing confirms that Grayson came in, but

> was extremely reticent as to the President's malady, giving no indication of any trouble other than a nervous breakdown. We decided that the Cabinet ought to meet and confer about the matter.[20]

It would be interesting to know where Tumulty got the idea that to determine the President was disabled would amount to ousting him. Was it from the Tyler precedent? The decision of the Garfield Cabinet? He mentions neither in his book. More likely the notion was Wilson's, not Tumulty's. The President was familiar with the history of the succession. As early as 1885, four years after Garfield's death, Wilson wrote that the importance of a Vice President came from the fact that "he may *cease to be*" Vice President.[21] It was a conviction that he reaffirmed as soon as he recovered: "When Lansing sought to oust me, I was upon my back. I am on my feet now and I will not have disloyalty about me."[22]

On February 10, 1920, Lansing told the Cabinet that the President had written to say he objected to Cabinet meetings being called except at his personal summons, and they were not to meet again unless Wilson personally convened them. Since October 6, 1919, they had met twenty-one times, and had sent Wilson memoranda of important discussions or decisions, but he had never indicated that he disapproved of the meetings. The President also taxed Lansing with having called the heads of executive departments into conference—and this, Wilson said, was an act none but the President had constitutional authority to perform. Lansing replied that he had met with department heads in regard to matters which could not be postponed until the President's recovery. He denied all thought of acting unconstitutionally or of assuming powers which belonged only to the President. On February 11, the President wrote characterizing Lansing's calling the Cabinet meetings as "an assumption of Presidential authority," and indicated that it was his pleasure that the Secretary of State resign. Lansing did so "with a sense of profound relief."[23] "Editorial comment and interviews with members of Congress show that Congress and the press supported Lansing almost unanimously."[24]

Although the President had by now recovered some of his power of decision and action, "he showed marked emotional instability, which made rational cooperation with his staff and his Cabinet almost impossible. After awhile, one after the other of his aides and Cabinet members could no longer take their chief's emotional outbursts and deserted him."[25]

And what were the Vice President's feelings as week after week went by with the country leaderless and uneasy with rumors? We know from Marshall's *Recollections* that

Those were not pleasant months for me. The standing joke of the country is that the only business of the vice-president is to ring the White House bell every morning and ask what is the state of health of the president. If there were a soul so lost to humanity as to have desired his death, I was not that soul. I hoped that he might acquire his wonted health. I was afraid to ask about it, for fear some censorious soul would accuse me of a longing for his place. I have never wanted his shoes. Peace, friendship and good will have ever been more to me than place or pomp or power.[26]

(To this catalog, the Vice President might fittingly have added that "good five-cent cigar" he declared the country was in need of—a remark which is likely to remain his sole bulwark against oblivion.) The "censorious soul" Marshall refers to could very well have been Tumulty, whose personal loyalty to the President obscured everything else. Tumulty and others of the White House circle, instead of looking to Marshall to lighten Wilson's burden, felt increasing antagonism toward him.[27]

So the government limped along, barely functioning for a year and a half. When Wilson finally did meet with the Cabinet, others took the initiative; his mind wandered and Mrs. Wilson stood by to call a halt when the President tired.[28] While the exact degree of Wilson's disability cannot be positively stated,

There can be no doubt concerning [his] inability to perform the duties of his office during much of the time after his collapse on September 25, 1919. . . . During the special session of the Sixty-sixth Congress twenty-eight acts of Congress became law because of the President's failure to pass on them within the requisite ten days. He did veto the Prohibition Enforcement Act on October 27, but from October 28 to November 18 he passed on only one of sixteen acts presented to him. He did not meet his Cabinet for eight months during his illness. The Senate Committee on Foreign Relations was unable to get action or information on the Shantung Settlement, a situation which caused Senator Albert B. Fall to suggest that if the President was too ill to discharge these duties, the Senate ought to recess until he was able to resume the responsibilities of his office. Although the Constitution says that the President shall receive the representatives of foreign states, . . . the British ambassador spent four months in Washington without seeing the President even once. . . .

Nearly every student of the period, whether scholar, Cabinet member, or journalist agrees that public business in general, and the Versailles Treaty in particular, was affected by the President's illness. In November of 1919 Senator Gilbert M. Hitchcock, the Democratic leader in the Senate, believed that he could get the Republicans to compromise on the treaty. But Wilson's physicians would not allow him to see the President. . . . Many feel that Wilson's isolation from public opinion, from his advisors, and from congressional leaders was one of the principal causes for defeat of the treaty.[29]

Mrs. Wilson and Dr. Grayson effectively protected the President from any problems which might cause anxiety; he lived out his term and achieved some measure of recovery. But there can be no doubt either that the national interest suffered or that the President's wife and his physician "did determine many questions of public policy . . . by deciding whom the President might and might not see, by deciding how long he might converse with those whom he was permitted to see, and by deciding what papers should be presented to him and what should not."[30]

Wilson accepted the loss of prestige and the failure of his dearest hopes with great dignity. His term of office ended on March 4, 1921, and he lived in retirement until his death on March 3, 1924.

3. TEMPORARY INABILITY AND THE TYLER PRECEDENT

The power vacuums during the illnesses of Garfield and Wilson were not primarily caused by the Tyler precedent. It was an element, certainly, in barring Arthur and Marshall from temporarily exercising the presidential powers and duties, but more than that it was a convenient smoke screen. After all, the Cabinet could scarcely be expected to announce that such-and-such steps were taken (or not taken) because the Vice President belonged to the wrong faction of the party, or because the President thought the Vice President was an intellectual nonentity, or because the two men disliked each other. And these were the true reasons for the Cabinet decisions in both the Garfield and Wilson cases. In both cases the governing conditions were the same: (1) a supposed threat to the President's program and thus to the political lives of the Cabinet members and (2) a conflict of personalities between the President and the Vice President. One condition resulted from the other; neither sprang full-fledged into being the instant the President was incapacitated. They had been latent for a long period of time, and the President's illness only brought them out into the open.

Wilson was incapacitated much longer than Garfield, and the question of presidential disability was considered by all three branches of government. Political motives were a deterrent to action by Congress. The Democrats, not wishing to publicize the President's illness any more than they had to, took no steps to secure the installation of Marshall as President; the Republicans saw the President's inability as an embarrassment to the Democrats and hoped for some scandalous disclosure—for example, that someone was forging Wilson's signature (which was rumored at one time). In any case, it was uncertain if Congress had the constitutional power to declare the President disabled.

There were other possible remedies. Vice President Marshall, upon whom presidential power devolved, might have undertaken to exercise this power and thereby have indirectly determined that Wilson was disabled. But Marshall refused to act as President. Some thought a writ of mandamus directing him to act as President was the answer. Although [a story appeared] in the *Christian Science Monitor* saying that the Supreme Court was ready and willing to issue such a writ, it is difficult to believe that the Court ever contemplated this. For the Supreme Court does not have original jurisdiction in such cases; and it is at least doubtful whether the question of inability is justiciable. The matter of Wilson's inability was actually brought up in courts once, but the courts did not take cognizance of it.[31]

Since the legislative branch, the judiciary, and the Vice President either would not or could not pass on the President's inability, that left the first step up to the Cabinet or the White House. The reasons for inaction already have been discussed in detail. In summary, usage had established the Tyler precedent, which transforms a Vice President into a President when the powers and duties of the higher office devolve upon him. But if the President were not dead but temporarily disabled when the powers and duties passed to the substitute President, then "either there must be two Presidents at once or the elected incumbent must be displaced. Since it is agreed that there cannot be another President until an elected President dies, resigns, or is removed, a disabled President's friends naturally have opposed any move to bring about the Vice President's succession."[32]

Henry E. Davis' discussion of this dilemma was written during Garfield's illness: it appeared in the *Congressional Record* while Wilson was incapacitated. Davis reviewed the wording of the original resolutions of the 1787 Constitutional Convention and the final draft which the delegates approved. In both cases, situations causing vacancy in office —death, resignation, removal from office (following impeachment), and inability—are grouped together. The first three are irreversible conditions: a President who is dead, or who has resigned, or who has been removed by impeachment obviously cannot resume office. Inability, on the other hand, is not necessarily permanent: a sick President may recover.

As the clause is worded, however, there is no apparent distinction between permanent and temporary inability. The status of the Vice President would seem to be the same whether the vacancy in the President's office is caused by death, resignation, removal by impeachment, or illness.

As Davis points out, this leaves unresolved the following questions:

What is inability in the sense of the provision; and what is its effect as to the Executive and the executive duties? Each of these questions includes another: Who shall decide when the inability occurs, whether it is continuing at a given date, when it has ceased? And, in case of inability of the President, does the Vice President become President or merely acting President for the time being? And at the termination of the inability shall the President and the Vice President resume their normal functions?[33]

That these questions exist is no reflection on the work of the framers of the Constitution. As Davis has demonstrated, the delegates were justified in thinking the inability provision "self-explanatory, self-operative, and sufficient."[34] But because it has repeatedly been construed on the basis of language alone, and without regard to the intent of the Constitutional Convention, there have been serious lapses in executive power, and the Tyler precedent "must today be regarded as having become the law of the land for those instances in which the President, through death, resignation, removal, or other cause, has disappeared from the scene."[35]

One of the most fascinating tricks of time—abetted by chauvinistic historians—is the way in which it magnifies the qualities of a nation's founding fathers. This is shown in the tendency to regard the men who drafted the Constitution as omniscient, and the Constitution itself as an inviolable body of sacred writings. But the delegates to the Federal Convention were under no such illusions. They knew that they were fallible human beings, not all-seeing gods, and they worked hard to make the Constitution flexible. "Interstate and foreign commerce," for example, is a concept broad enough to be applied to jet transportation as well as travel by barge and clipper. But it was impossible to anticipate the radical changes the years would bring, and the drafters of the Constitution looked to their descendants to adapt the basic instrument to new situations and new conditions. Had they intended otherwise, no means of amendment would have been provided.

Veneration for the Constitution which blindly ignores this fact, or which consists of worshiping the word and ignoring the intent, is at best a poor compliment to our forefathers; and it becomes the reverse of a virtue when it is made the excuse for avoiding responsible action. When the Garfield and Wilson Cabinets were confronted with the problem of temporary presidential inability, they refused to consider adapting the constitutional provision to meet an emergency for which it supplied no specific directive. Lacking the moral stamina and the intellectual stature to withstand political pressure and to look beyond the exigencies of the moment, they gratefully reverted to the Tyler precedent—a ready-made alibi for inaction.

Chapter IV

Mr. President, How Is Your Health?

An aspect of presidential inability highlighted during President Wilson's illness concerns the importance of trustworthy information about the Chief Executive's health. The atmosphere of secrecy that enveloped the White House during the "Mrs. Wilson Regency" was responsible for swarms of dark rumors about the nature of the President's illness. Radio, television, and the keyhole columnist had not yet come into being, but even so the stories reached every corner of the country. "The less the public knew, the more gossip was invented. It was whispered that the President had a venereal disease, even that he was insane. The rumor in medical circles was that Wilson's left knee had been deformed by Charcot's disease, a consequence of locomotor ataxia."*[1] At the very least, such stories are an embarrassment to the administration, impair national morale, and lend aid and comfort to our enemies.

1. PRESIDENT CLEVELAND HAS A TOOTH OUT

In attempts to justify withholding information about the President's health, it is customary to cite the case of President Grover Cleveland. Soon after he was inaugurated in 1893, the country was gripped by a major financial panic. The gold reserve had dropped below a hundred million dollars, national and state banks were failing, and on June 27 the bottom fell out of the stock market. It was thought— and written—that "Mr. Cleveland is about all that stands between this country and absolute disaster." On June 30, as part of his major strategy in fighting inflation, the President summoned an extra session of Congress to convene on August 7, at which time he would request the repeal of the Sherman Silver Act.

---

*Locomotor ataxia is a chronic disease of the nervous system, which often results from syphilis.

At this moment, when the curtain was about to rise upon a battle royal in Congress, there occurred one of the dramatic minor episodes of American history. The whole strength of the assault upon the Sherman silver-purchase clauses lay, as everyone realized, in the grim determination of Cleveland's purpose. His weight of character could force enough members of his party into line, and nothing else could. Even temporary incapacitation might be fatal to his aims, while if any accident suddenly removed him from the scene, all would be lost; for the Vice President, Adlai E. Stevenson, would infallibly bring the nation to the silver standard. [Stevenson had secured the vice presidential nomination as a sop to the silverites.] An unhappier time for the development of a dangerous malady was hardly conceivable. Yet on May 5 Cleveland discovered a rough spot on the roof of his mouth. It gave him increasing discomfort, and on June 18 he had it examined by the White House physician, Dr. O'Reilly. The latter found a malignant growth as large as a quarter of a dollar. . . . An immediate operation was imperative. Yet it had to be kept a complete secret, for the knowledge that Cleveland's life was in danger would have precipitated a new and far greater panic. The most urgent work on the President's desk was hastily dispatched. Dr. [Joseph D.] Bryant took complete charge of the case, writing [Secretary of War Daniel S.] Lamont that he could not assume the responsibility for any delay until even August 1st if the growth progressed as it commonly did in such cases.[2]

On the evening of June 30, the same day that he issued his call to Congress, President Cleveland boarded Commodore E. C. Benedict's yacht *Oneida,* anchored in New York's East River. The crew had been told that he was to have two teeth extracted, and an operating room had been prepared in the below-deck salon. Here, on July 1, while the yacht cruised slowly in Long Island Sound, the President underwent surgery to remove a cancerous growth from his jaw. The entire operation was done from within the mouth, so as to leave no external scar. All went well and on July 5 the President went to his summer home to recuperate. But it was feared that not all the cancerous tissue had been removed. A second operation was necessary; it took place on July 17, also on board the *Oneida.* Equipped with an artificial jaw, the President kept his date with Congress on August 7. The story did not become public knowledge for more than twenty years.[3]

It is hard to quarrel with success, yet even though the gamble came off this is not to say that it was the wisest course. If the President had failed to survive the operation, his death in such melodramatic, cloak-and-daggerish circumstances—aboard the yacht of a plutocrat—would have been far more demoralizing to the nation than if the public had been kept informed. It should be noted, moreover, that neither the Vice President nor any member of the Cabinet except Lamont knew anything of the real situation, let alone being provided with the briefing necessary to insure the continuation of orderly processes of government.*

In fairness to Cleveland, however, it must be remembered that in 1893 news coverage of the President was not nearly so intensive as it has since become. In our day Washington is teeming with people who are concerned, directly or indirectly, with collecting and disseminating the news. As well as accredited reporters for newspapers, magazines, radio and television networks, and other communications media, there is a whole host of subcategories—publicity men, professional tipsters, lobbyists, and representatives of private business and of special interest groups. In addition, there is the large segment of the capital's population (at a rough estimate, just about everybody) who wish to appear "in the know" for prestige reasons and who can repeat or even invent a story without any fear that they will be held to account for it.

The lives of people in high places always are a subject of gossip and speculation, and usually the speed with which

---

*"I can't recall precisely any conversations bearing on . . . the relations of Grandfather and Grover Cleveland at the time of the latter's operation. . . . Relations with Cleveland and his family were always very cordial and friendly, and, I had assumed, intimate. . . . But I can recall nothing specific about any briefing at the time of Cleveland's operation. Indeed, I was rather under the impression that no one knew about it, including most of his cabinet" (Adlai E. Stevenson to Richard H. Hansen, April 26, 1962. See also Nevins, *Grover Cleveland*, pp. 532–533, and Nevins [ed.], *The Letters of Grover Cleveland*, p. 370).

rumors about them spread is in direct ratio to the sensational or scurrile character of their content. In respect to the President's activities, and particularly his health, the least suggestion of a mystery—any hint that not all the cards are on the table, that news is being withheld—becomes a cue for rumor-mongers to swing into action. The death of President Wilson's successor, Warren G. Harding, is a case in point.

2. "THE STRANGE DEATH OF PRESIDENT HARDING"

By the summer of 1923, the third of President Harding's administration, it was becoming uncomfortably apparent that the highest office in the land had been bestowed on a man wholly unqualified to hold it. The exposure of the venality and corrupt practices of a cluster of Harding's free-wheeling associates already had begun, and details of the President's private life—his speculations on the stock market, his gambling and drinking, rumors of a mistress and an illegitimate daughter—were openly circulated in many quarters. But it was not generally known that the President's health had been poor for more than a year. Except when he was flat on his back, the President was always represented to the public as the picture of health.[4]

In January of 1922, Harding had been seriously ill with what was diagnosed as influenza, but probably was an unrecognized attack of coronary thrombosis. Dr. Emmanuel Libmann, the famed heart specialist and diagnostician, met the President at a dinner party in the fall of that year; he subsequently told a friend that in his opinion the President was "suffering from a disease of the coronary arteries of the heart and would be dead in six months." Actually, it was eight.

On June 20, 1923, the President and Mrs. Harding left for a trip to Alaska. On July 28, while in Seattle on their return trip to Washington, the President had a severe seizure which was diagnosed as cardiac by Commander Joel T. Boone of the Navy Medical Corps, one of the three doctors in the President's entourage. However, Dr. Boone was outranked by Brigadier General Charles T. Sawyer, Surgeon General of the United States and a personal friend of the President's. Sawyer diagnosed the illness as an "acute gastro-intestinal attack," probably caused by "crabmeat-copper pto-maine poisoning," and this is what the official bulletin said, although as it happened the President had not eaten any crabmeat.

In view of this diagnosis, the President was permitted to get up and no strict bed rest was enforced. Three days later in San Francisco he had another seizure. Two more physicians were called in, and the diagnosis was now broncho-pneumonia and circulatory collapse. At last, bed rest was made mandatory.

On August 2, all perceptible symptoms of the sickness seemed to have disappeared. The President was in better spirits than he had been for a long time, and at 4:30 P.M. the doctors gave out an optimistic bulletin. At 7:30 P.M., while Mrs. Harding was reading to the President, a "convulsive tremor" passed over his face, his body shuddered and sagged, and he was dead.

The official bulletin, signed by the physicians in attendance, stated that "we all believe he died from apoplexy or the rupture of a blood vessel in the axis of the brain near the respiratory center." However, the medical evidence indicated coronary thrombosis as the probable cause of death, although this cannot be stated with certainty, since Mrs. Harding refused to permit an autopsy.

Suicide and venereal disease figured in the word-of-mouth "inside stories" that flooded the country immediately after the President's death. Mrs. Harding's refusal to permit an autopsy and the bewildering variety of diagnoses which figured in the official bulletins—hypertension, angina pectoris, acute gastrointestinal attack, crabmeat-copper poisoning, gall bladder disease, pneumonia, circulatory collapse, apoplexy—undoubtedly encouraged speculation and abetted the spread of rumors. Other contributing factors were the suddenness of the President's death and the image-makers' projection of him to the public as a man bursting with health.

The most despicable of the stories about the President's

death—that he had been poisoned by his wife—appeared in *The Strange Death of President Harding*, by Gaston B. Means, a former Department of Justice employee who had been forced to resign his job because of his involvement in some of the many government scandals of the ill-fated Harding administration.[5] Eighteen years later a similar title was employed for a no less scabrous and irresponsible attack on Franklin D. Roosevelt, and again it was lack of reliable information about the President's health which provided the author with an opening.

3. ROOSEVELT, THE PRESS, AND THE PALACE GUARD

Because he had been crippled as a result of poliomyelitis, President Roosevelt's health was a national issue even before he took office in 1932. The general and deep admiration for his triumph over a disability which would have ended the career of most men made it infeasible for his political opponents to attempt making political capital of his disability during Roosevelt's first two administrations. Nor did the question of his fitness enter appreciably into the 1940 third-term campaign. However, in a book published after the President's death, Secretary of the Interior Frances Perkins quoted Roosevelt as saying to labor leader Daniel Tobin that he couldn't run for a third term because "I am tired. I really am. . . . This sinus trouble I've got, the Washington climate makes it dreadful. . . . The doctors say I have to go into the hospital for a month of steady treatment. But I can't do that, you know. When a President does that, the bottom drops out of the stock market, the Japs take advantage of what they think is serious illness, the Germans start propaganda that I am dying and that the United States is in a panic. No, I can't be President again. I have to get over this sinus."[6]

After Pearl Harbor, wartime secrecy tended to isolate the President from the press, and the result was the growth of some fantastic stories about his last years in office and his death. Following the Teheran Conference (November 28—December 1, 1943), rumors of illness and of physical deterioration owing to the unprecedented length of Roosevelt's term in office began to make noticeable headway, and these stories appear to have had some factual basis. According to Judge Samuel I. Rosenman, Roosevelt's friend and associate from 1928 until his death:

The President developed some sort of bronchial affliction at Teheran which gave him a racking cough. . . . The [doctors] found no unusual condition for a man of his age except his cough and his sinuses. While Teheran was a high point in the President's career as Commander-in-Chief of our armed forces and as our leader in foreign affairs, it seemed to me also the turning point of his physical career. I think that his physical decline can be dated from Teheran, although at the time we did not see it.[7]

From early in January, 1944, until his death on April 12, 1945, the President's health seems to have been a source of continuing anxiety to the White House circle, and rumors proliferated all during this period. Immediately after the President's death, John Gunther has recorded, stories began to circulate

some of which are still heard today—that FDR had shot himself, that he had been shot, that he had fallen off a cliff, and even that he didn't die, but had been packed off to a sanitarium as a mental cripple. . . .

Mainly the attempt to make a mystery out of Roosevelt's death is of political derivation. Critics strive to prove (a) that he was much sicker than he ever was; (b) that he should not have been allowed to run for a fourth term, considering his condition; (c) that members of a White House camarilla concealed the true facts from the public, and foisted a dying Roosevelt on the country out of their own ambition and greed for power.

Among the ailments the President was variously supposed to have been suffering from were "coronary thrombosis, a brain hemorrhage, a nervous breakdown, an aneurism of the aorta, and a cancerous prostate." Also "reports" were repeatedly heard that he had been spirited off to the Mayo Clinic for an operation for a malignant tumor of the liver or rectum. . . .

Admiral [Ross T.] McIntire, who had been Roosevelt's doctor for many years, vigorously refutes these charges. The

President, he insists, was in good enough health for the proper discharge of all his duties to the end. McIntire takes full note of the frequent sinus attacks, the debilitating bout of bronchitis and intestinal influenza in 1944, and the pallor, fatigue, and loss of weight, but he denies strenuously that any of this had any critical importance. . . .

Questions about the President's health became so widespread, particularly during the fourth-term campaign, that McIntire issued several statements denying rumors and attesting to his good health. On October 12, 1944, for instance, he stated flatly, "The President's health is perfectly OK. There are absolutely no organic difficulties at all." . . .[8]

As Robert E. Sherwood, among others, has noted, the one serious issue in the 1944 campaign was the President's health.

There was a good deal of extremely ugly whispering. . . . When he made his acceptance speech before his departure for the Pacific tour in July, a photograph had been taken in which he appeared haggard, glassy eyed and querulous—and this photograph had been given a very wide advertisement in the press and in the pamphlets with which the Republicans were flooding the country. On his return from the Pacific trip, Roosevelt had made a nation-wide broadcast from the Bremerton Navy Yard at Seattle; when he delivered this speech he wore his leg braces for, I believe, the first time since he had returned from Cairo and Teheran and he was in such pain that he had to support himself by holding on to the lectern . . . which made it extremely difficult for him to turn the pages of his reading copy and made the speech sound faltering and uncertain. . . . It was significant that, after this speech, the public opinion polls indicated a sudden and ominous slump for Roosevelt and a consequent rise in Dewey's stock.

Sherwood also notes that, although he had heard Roosevelt had lost a lot of weight, "I was unprepared for the almost ravaged appearance of his face. He had his coat off and his shirt collar seemed several sizes too large for his emaciated neck. But I soon began to suspect that the fears expressed by Hopkins, Watson and the others were groundless. He seemed to be more full of good humor and of fight than ever." Again, referring to the "innumerable baseless and incredibly malicious rumors," Sherwood says,

but there was some visible support for them—for [the President] was now truly crippled. The frail muscles in his legs and hips had become flabby through long disuse in the months between Teheran and the Bremerton speech, during which time he had made no public appearances at which he would have to stand up—and he never wore the painful braces except on such necessary public occasions. It was now felt that he would probably never again be able to stand up and walk. . . . Actually, during the weeks of this campaign, he did manage to regain the use of his legs sufficiently to be able to stand up and speak from the back platform of his train for as long as half an hour. . . .[9]

Because of the secrecy sometimes surrounding the President's whereabouts—a necessary security measure in wartime —rumors that he had been hospitalized were lent a certain plausibility, and in the spring of 1944 on one occasion even members of the White House press corps were taken in. The story is related by Mike Reilly, then head of the White House Secret Service detail:

The Boss's so-called illness and heart attacks were a source of great unhappiness to him. He thought the stories had been printed for political purposes and were outrageous lies, which worried his family and weakened his position in dealing with some of the rugged characters with whom he had to dicker at home and abroad. Right now—and FDR needs no help today from anyone, particularly the likes of me—I will swear on everything I love or believe that the Boss never had a heart attack and that he never was seriously ill in the ten years that I worked at his side until the day of his death.

Knowing how the Boss felt about these stories and realizing that there were three honest reporters who really believed he was in a hospital somewhere, I decided to forestall any newspaper junk that would upset FDR on this desperately needed vacation [at Bernard Baruch's plantation in South Carolina]. So I said to the reporters, "Will you believe he's here if you see him yourselves?"

"Sure."

"Will your bosses believe it and keep quiet if you tell

them these wires they are shooting down here are sheer bunk?"

"Yes."

"Okay," I said, "be ready at ten tomorrow and you'll see him."

They were picked up at ten and taken to the estate. 1 knew the President would pass a certain spot at eleven, so I parked the cars under some trees at the side of the road and waited. Sure enough, he went by on time and the reporters saw him.

"He looks tired," one said.

"He is. That's why I brought you guys out here. He's tired all right, but he's not in any Boston or Chicago hospital. Tell that to your bosses."[10]

However, although Elliott Roosevelt has declared categorically that "there is no evidence of any kind, either in [President Roosevelt's] medical history or in the knowledge of any member of his family or those who were close to him throughout his years in the White House, to support any theory that he had suffered from heart attacks or cerebral hemorrhages at any time before his death,"[11] this statement is apparently contradicted by two incidents recounted by James Roosevelt in his book *Affectionately, F.D.R.* The first incident occurred in the fall of 1944:

I was temporarily stationed at Camp Pendleton, near San Diego, California, as intelligence officer. . . . Father paid us a visit to review a landing exercise being staged by the Fifth Marine Division as a dress rehearsal for its next Pacific operation.

Just before we were to leave for the exercise, Father turned suddenly white, his face took on an agonized look, and he said to me: "Jimmy, I don't know if I can make it— I have horrible pains." It was a struggle for him to get the words out.

I was so scared I did not know what to think or do. I gripped his hand and felt his forehead. We considered calling the doctor, then decided against it. Both of us thought he was suffering from some digestive upset—Father himself was positive it had nothing to do with his heart. We talked some more, and I told him that, if he possibly could summon the strength, he should try not to cancel his appearance at the exercise, as it would create much alarm.

"Yes," Pa said, almost sighing, "it would be very bad. But help me out of my berth and let me stretch out flat on the deck awhile—that may help."

So for perhaps ten minutes, while I kept as quiet as possible, Father lay on the floor of the railroad car, his eyes closed, his face drawn, his powerful torso occasionally convulsed as the waves of pain stabbed him. Never in my life had I felt so alone with him—and so helpless.

Then he opened his eyes, exhaled deeply, and said: "Help me up now, Jimmy." I did so. I helped him to get ready and the Commander-in-Chief went out to review the exercises.

The second attack took place after Roosevelt's fourth inaugural, January 20, 1945:

The first moment I saw Father I realized something was terribly wrong. He looked awful and regardless of what the doctors said, I knew in my heart that his days were numbered. Just before he proceeded to the reception in the State Dining Room Father and I were alone for a few minutes in the Green Room. He was thoroughly chilled, and the same type of pain, though somewhat less acute, that had bothered him in San Diego, was stabbing him again. He gripped my arm hard and said: "Jimmy, I can't take this unless you get me a stiff drink." I said I would and as I started out he called to me: "You'd better make it straight." I brought him a tumbler full of whisky which he drank as if it were medicine. In all my life I had never seen Father take a drink in that manner. Then he went on to the reception and no one there—no one but me—knew how he felt.[12]

But even though "no one . . . knew how he felt"—and the above account implies that the President never informed Dr. McIntire of his symptoms—nonetheless, a number of people seem to have noticed that the President was failing. His secretary, Grace Tully, writing of the fourth-term inauguration, said:

Several close acquaintances of the President have since said or written that they were distressed by his appearance on that inauguration day. I am sure that those who did not see him daily would be more aware of the change over a period of time. . . . I had been disturbed by the signs of fatigue shown by the Boss but to me the greatest and most serious bits of evidence did not appear until his return from Yalta.[13]

Vice President Truman, meeting Roosevelt on his return from Yalta, was disturbed by his appearance, but "after the first shock of seeing [him], I tried to dismiss from my mind the ominous thoughts of a possible breakdown, counting on his ability to bounce back from the stresses and strains of office."[14] Secretary of State Edward R. Stettinius, Jr., in his book about the Yalta conference, says that it seemed to him "some kind of deterioration had taken place in the President's health between the middle of December and the inauguration on January 20," though he is careful to state that at Yalta (February 1-3), Roosevelt's mind "functioned with clarity and conciseness, furnishing excellent proof that he was alert and in full command of his faculties."[15] As John Gunther points out, the President's condition "varied sharply from day to day; he always picked up and bounced back quickly" and this as much as anything accounts for the discrepancies and varying views expressed in the many accounts of the President's last months.

... his inner vitality, even though weakened, was so radiant that ... he could make almost any visitor completely forget that he seemed ill. ... Many people who knew him well, including those who tried to build a kind of protective screen around him, had come to think in a peculiar way that he was indestructible. Life was inconceivable without Roosevelt as President: ... it was just not possible that he could be sick enough to die.[16]

When death did come it was with such swiftness that the problem of keeping the Vice President notified of the President's condition did not arise; Stephen Early, the Presidential Press Secretary, did not try to reach him until the President was dead. Truman, who consulted frequently with Roosevelt about the legislative program, was aware of his physical decline—"I saw what the long years in the presidency had done to him."[17] But still the news was so unexpected, he felt as if "the whole weight of the moon and stars" had fallen on him. The Vice President, no more than the White House inner circle, seems to have apprehended that the President might actually die. They preferred to believe the reassuring medical reports rather than their own eyes.*

James Roosevelt's account of his father's attacks of "indigestion" underlines the necessity for keeping the President's physicians informed of his condition. When the President of the United States has pains of the severity described, while it may be an act of stoical courage to bear them in silence it is also a shocking failure of responsibility to the government not to speak out. If Dr. McIntire had known the facts at the time, he would have insisted on an immediate examination; there would have been an opportunity for diagnosis and treatment. But a doctor cannot diagnose something the patient is silent about. In fairness to the Vice President also, the President should be frank about his condition. But Harry Truman wrote that

the only indication I had ever had that [President Roosevelt] knew he was none too well was when he talked to me just before I set out on my campaign trip for the vice-presidency in 1944. He asked me how I was going to travel, and I told him I intended to cover the country by airplane. "Don't do that, please," he told me. "Go by train. It is necessary that you take care of yourself."

The sources cited thus far have been taken from the writings of men and women who deeply admired the President and in most cases, were closely associated with him. Representative of the "hearsay type" of account is one by Karl C. Wold, M.D., which appeared in *Look*. Titled "The Truth about F.D.R.'s Health," it included the statement:

---

*A. Merriman Smith, dean of the White House press corps, who saw the President daily, wrote of the press conferences, "We saw Franklin D. Roosevelt die over a period of about a year." Quoted in Edgar Eugene Robinson, *The Roosevelt Leadership, 1933–1945* (Philadelphia and New York: J. B. Lippincott Co., 1955), p. 327 n.

As this book is being revised for the printer, a UPI story datelined Washington reports that according to a new biography of Harry S. Truman, *The Man from Missouri*, by Alfred Steinberg, "Democratic party members were convinced as early as January 1944 that Roosevelt was showing unmistakable signs of failing health. . . . Steinberg quotes Truman as saying the thought of succeeding Roosevelt in office 'scares the hell out of me'" (*Lincoln Evening Journal*, April 17, 1962, 3:1–2).

In the later summer of 1938, while Roosevelt was visiting a son, James, at the Mayo Clinic, in Rochester, Minn., the first of a series of strokes occurred. The attack was light and the hemorrhage evidently small because recovery was quick and complete.

Under the subheads "Second Stroke" and "Third Stroke," the article further implied that the President had suffered a stroke following his trip to Teheran in December, 1943, and another on March 25, 1945.[18]

A reply to this article, "They're Lying about F.D.R.'s Health," by Elliott Roosevelt, appeared in *Liberty*. After citing good and sufficient evidence to demonstrate that the Wold article was "completely false in every respect," Roosevelt reported a telephone conversation with Dr. Wold shortly after the *Look* article appeared. Dr. Wold said that his article had been "highly sensationalized by the magazine and much of the material that appears in my book [*Mr. President—How Is Your Health?*, the medical histories of the Presidents] has been omitted, giving rise to a completely false impression as to the intent of my writings." As to the sources of his information, about the three alleged strokes,

he said that he had a hazy recollection that he had received much of the information in a letter from Walter Trohan a Washington correspondent who had been with the President on those occasions. . . . [Elliott Roosevelt pointed out that] Mr. Trohan is the Washington correspondent of the Chicago *Tribune*, the most anti-Roosevelt paper in the United States. Mr. Trohan collaborated with James A. Farley in Mr. Farley's book attacking Franklin D. Roosevelt and his policies. . . . Needless to say, he was at no time a White House confidant and wasn't regarded as an intimate of the President. . . .*[19]

*Dr. Wold is now dead, but it has been alleged by a businessman friend of his that Mrs. Roosevelt and one of her sons were so incensed by Wold's book that they went out to St. Paul, Minnesota, to sue Wold and his publisher, but changed their minds after they had talked with Dr. Wold and seen his evidence. Queried about this story, Mrs. Roosevelt replied that she had never seen Dr. Wold and had never gone to St. Paul for the purpose of suing him and his publisher (Mrs. Franklin D. Roosevelt to Richard H. Hansen, December 19, 1961).

The Strange Death of Franklin D. Roosevelt: A History of the Roosevelt-Delano Dynasty, America's Royal Family has as its theme that the President was the stooge of an aristocratic, imperialistic dynasty.[20] At Teheran, so the author tells us, the waiter assigned to the President and to Prime Minister Churchill was actually "a physician who specialized in the science of poisoning, toxicology. . . . Shortly after their departure Winston Churchill became extremely ill. He was hurried to Egypt where . . . his death was expected momentarily. But his life was saved by a protege of his, Sir Arthur Fleming, the discoverer of penicillin . . . Roosevelt also was extremely ill on his return. He was unable to walk or stand unassisted, and never recovered his strength. His disability bore a striking resemblance to poisoning with a form of curare, an Indian arrow poison that had engaged the interest of Russian scientists. He wasted steadily thereafter." The author lists eight other possible causes of the President's death, including cancer.

It goes without saying that this vicious and absurd mishmash is wholly undocumented. Like the Wold article, it is mentioned here only as an example of the type of material bred by secrecy or incomplete information about the President's health.

The most recent case of prolonged presidential inability occurred during the administration of Dwight D. Eisenhower, and for the first time in American history the public was kept well informed of the President's condition. Eisenhower had been a young Army captain during Wilson's long ordeal; he had heard the ugly rumors which flooded the country at that time and had seen the nation floundering leaderless through the crucial treaty-making period after World War I. He had been a General of the Army when President Roosevelt's health was the subject of anxious speculation in capitals and headquarters all over the European Theater of Operations; with millions of others, he had felt the shock, experienced the same moment of stunned disbelief, when news of the Commander in Chief's death was flashed around the world. A decade later, as President of the United States, Eisenhower was struck down by illness.

Mindful of the Wilson and Roosevelt episodes, he did everything he could to make certain that the facts about his condition were immediately communicated to the public and to insure that the power and duties of the Presidency were exercised without interruption.

4. THE THREE EISENHOWER CRISES

When President Eisenhower's seizure of September 24, 1955, was diagnosed as a heart attack, the whole world shook with the vibrations of the needle on the electrocardiograph. The United States, by virtue of its regional alliances as well as its membership in the United Nations, had ties in every quarter of the globe. More than that, it was the leader and mainstay of free peoples everywhere; what happened here would have a direct bearing on their destiny.

The domestic reaction to the President's illness was reflected by the stock market: on September 26, the first trading day after the news broke, prices lost over twelve billion dollars in values. Despite the assurance of the "assistant president," Sherman Adams, that there was no government business requiring immediate presidential attention, the *New York Times* reported on September 27 that "top-level decisions were pending on disarmament policy, budgetary problems, military force levels, certain politico-strategic questions, withdrawal of troops from Korea, future military policy toward Formosa and reduction of forces in Japan."[21]

The attack occurred when the President was in Denver, a guest at his mother-in-law's home. About 2:30 A.M. on September 24, he awakened in severe pain. Mrs. Eisenhower called Major General Howard Snyder, the President's physician, who arrived about 3:00 A.M. and administered emergency treatment, including drugs to relieve the pain. At 7:00 A.M. he called Murray Snyder, the Assistant Presidential Press Secretary, who was also in Denver, and left word that the President had indigestion and to cancel his appointments. When the President awoke at 12:30 P.M., Dr. Snyder called Fitzsimmons Army Hospital and asked that an electrocardiograph be brought around. The cardiogram, which showed a lesion on the anterior wall of the heart, confirmed Dr. Snyder's original diagnosis of coronary thrombosis. Murray Snyder was then informed, and after the President had been taken to Fitzsimmons Hospital the news was released to the press.

In a subsequent report to the White House, Dr. Snyder had this to say about the eleven-hour delay in communicating the news:

It was difficult for me to assume the responsibility of refraining from making public immediately the diagnosis of coronary thrombosis. I postponed public announcement because I wished the President to benefit from the rest and quiet induced by the sedation incident to combating the initial manifestations. This decision also spared him, his wife and mother-in-law emotional upset upon too precipitate announcement of such serious import. This action, I believe, limited the heart damage to a minimum and enabled us to confirm the diagnosis by cardiogram and make an unhurried transference from home to hospital.[22]

The decision to release the facts was made by James E. Hagerty, the President's Press Secretary, who was in Washington but flew at once to Denver and took charge at the Summer White House. As soon as the doctors would allow it, Hagerty saw the President, who approved his action in releasing the news and told him to "give 'em the facts."[23]

In Washington, Vice President Richard Nixon conferred with the Acting Attorney General, William P. Rogers (Attorney General Herbert Brownell was out of the country), and later with Secretary of State Foster Dulles and other members of the Cabinet. They were told that Colonel Thomas M. Mattingly, Chief of Cardiology at Walter Reed Army Hospital, was on his way to Denver with a plane-load of doctors. Although they "had nothing against military doctors . . . [they] could not overlook that many people in the country might have more confidence, however unwarranted, in a civilian heart specialist of national reputation." Dr. Paul Dudley White, a pioneer in cardiology, was suggested by several people, among them Secretary of the Treasury George Humphrey, and General Wilton B. Persons, the Deputy Assistant to the President, was given the "delicate and difficult task" of convincing Dr. Snyder that no slight was intended by calling in Dr. White on consultation. Once this matter of professional etiquette had been satisfactorily resolved, the Vice President and the Cabinet could give some thought to the problem of "how to carry on in [the President's] absence without allowing the government to drift dangerously in foreign or domestic affairs. There is an old political axiom that where a vacuum exists, it will be filled by the nearest or strongest power. That had to be avoided at all costs."[24]

On Sunday, September 25, the Vice President was told Dr. White's prognosis that barring complications the President would be well enough to take on limited duties within two weeks and to resume normal activities within two months.

Fortunately, this was vacation time in the government when there was a lull in the usual rush of activities. Several long-range projects were under way, like preparation of the budget and the State of the Union message, but there seemed to be no pressing item that required presidential action. Congress was in adjournment; there was no pending legislation. The cold war seemed frozen for the moment. . . .

We were fairly certain by this time that there was nothing requiring the President's signature or attention which could not be delayed for two weeks. The significance of this was that it became apparent this early that we would not have to solve the thorny problem of a delegation of the President's constitutional powers.[25]

The President's right-hand man, Sherman Adams, was in Scotland at the time of the attack, but was back in Washington by Monday, September 26. No Cabinet meeting was called, as was done in the Wilson case. Vice President Nixon came to a luncheon meeting with the senior staff personnel of the White House and afterward conferred with Adams. That night there was a meeting at the home of Acting Attorney General Rogers, attended by the Vice President, Adams, General Persons, Leonard Hall (the Republican National Chairman), and Hall's press aide, Lou Guylay. The meeting was devoted chiefly to the political questions which would inevitably result from the President's illness—for example, would he or would he not be able to run for a second term?

In view of Dr. White's encouraging report and since there was no government business requiring immediate presidential attention, Nixon, Adams, and the other members of the administrative team aimed to carry on in a "business as usual" atmosphere. On Thursday, September 29, the National Security Council held its regular meeting, presided over by the Vice President; he had previously presided at council meetings when the President was away from Washington. Twenty-three ranking members of the administration

. . . spent considerable time putting somewhat of an official stamp of approval on the course of action for the interim government. It was officially decided, for instance, that Sherman Adams should go to Denver to serve as liaison and administrative assistant to the President, while Jerry Persons would handle the paper work at the President's White House office, routing the documents which the President should see through Adams.[26]

When he arrived in Denver, "Adams made it clear to the attending physicians that he would defer to their judgment on bringing matters to Eisenhower's attention during the crucial seven days ahead."[27] Adams already had made up his mind that his course of action with the President—what he was consulted on, or told—would depend to a great extent on Dr. White's advice, and had so informed the members of the Cabinet before his plane trip to Colorado. During the remainder of the period during which it was possible for complications to arise, Adams and Hagerty met daily with Dr. White and his associates to discuss what work was to be placed before the President.[28]

For the next two months the government was managed by a six-man committee made up of Vice President Nixon, Secretary of State Dulles, Attorney General Brownell, Secretary of the Treasury Humphrey, General Persons, and Adams. Nixon, according to Adams, "leaned over backward to avoid any appearance of assuming presidential authority," but though things went fairly smoothly, Adams and all the members of the committee knew that at any moment a global crisis or national emergency could make this "government by community understanding" woefully inadequate.[29] As Vice President Nixon later wrote:

Although it was hardly mentioned, I am certain that many of us realized our team-government would be inadequate to handle an international crisis, such as a brush-fire war or an internal uprising in a friendly country or a crisis of an ally. The ever-present possibility of an attack on the United States was always hanging over us. Would the President be well enough to make the decision? If not, who had the authority to push the button?[30]

It was only at the end of the two-week period, during which the scar tissue in the President's heart had formed, that the tension in Washington slackened.

After his recovery from the heart attack, President Eisenhower continued in good health until early in June, 1956, when he had an attack of ileitis, a blockage of the lower part of the small intestine. Shortly after midnight on June 8, his condition became acute and the team of doctors at Walter Reed Hospital decided on immediate surgery. From 2:30 to 4:35 A.M., Adams, Hagerty, and Andrew Goodpaster, the President's staff secretary, kept vigil outside the operating room. The surgeons found no sign of malignancy; the President's recovery was quick and uneventful. However,

the surgery focused the President's attention on the legal problems of the disability of a Chief Executive. . . . On several occasions afterwards, he pointed out to Vice President Nixon that for the two hours he was under anesthesia the country was without a Chief Executive, the armed forces without a Commander-in-Chief. In the event of a national emergency during those two hours, who would have had the authority to act for a completely disabled President? . . . He told some of those around him that if illness ever struck again and he felt he could not physically carry on the burdens of office, he would resign.[31]

Seventeen months later, on the afternoon of November 27, 1957, Ann Whitman, the President's personal secretary, went to Sherman Adams "on the verge of tears." She was upset over an incident which had just occurred in the President's office—"He tried to tell me something but he couldn't express himself. Something seemed to have happened to him all of a sudden." When Mrs. Whitman called Dr. Snyder, the President refused to leave his desk. "Go away from me," he tried to say. Goodpaster finally persuaded him to leave his office and walk back to the living quarters.[32]

Dr. Snyder persuaded the President to go to bed; it was his opinion that the President had suffered a stroke and a neurologist was called to the White House. There was a state dinner scheduled for King Mohammed V of Morocco, and while Adams was discussing this complication with Mrs. Eisenhower the President got out of bed, and insisted that he intended to go to the dinner. But he still had a noticeable speech impediment, and Adams and Dr. Snyder managed to dissuade him. Despite his insistence to the contrary, according to Adams, the President knew something was wrong with himself: "He became upset and impatient with his difficulty in seizing the word that he wanted to say, sometimes coming out with a word or syllable that had no relation to the word he had in his mind."[33]

Adams called Vice President Nixon to the White House and related what had happened. He told Nixon: "This is a terribly, terribly difficult thing to handle. You may be President in the next twenty-four hours." It was decided to withhold any announcement that the President had suffered a stroke until Dr. Snyder's original diagnosis had been confirmed. A bulletin was issued stating that the President had suffered a chill. Although Mrs. Eisenhower was greatly distressed, she realized that canceling the state dinner would alarm the nation and it was held as scheduled.[34]

On the next morning—Tuesday—a meeting was held at the White House. At that time, says Sherman Adams, "the doctors could not tell us how seriously the shock of the previous day had affected the President's nervous system or whether it might be the first in a series of more damaging strokes."[35] Nixon also agrees that the tension

seemed even greater than at the time of the heart attack. In contrast to that period in 1955, this was the worst time possible for the President to be incapacitated. It was a time of international tensions. Only a month before the Soviet Union had put its first Sputnik in orbit, and the whole structure of America's military might and scientific technology was under suspicion here and abroad. The most immediate problem was a scheduled meeting of the North Atlantic Treaty Organization only three weeks away. . . . On the domestic front, the first signs of the 1958 economic recession were becoming obvious. . . . We were having serious budget problems. . . . the government had borrowed up to its legal debt limit, and we had to prepare the fiscal 1959 budget with still higher defense spending. The Administration also had to complete its legislative program, the State of the Union message, the budget and economic messages for the opening days of Congress in January.[36]

The medical report passed along to the press—that the President had suffered a "mild" stroke which affected only his ability to speak, and that his mind and reasoning powers were not involved—got a quite different reaction from the public than the news about the heart attack. "During the heart attack, the nation worried if the President would live or die but not about his ability to carry on if he recovered. This was not the case during the stroke. The public seemed to say okay, he may get well, but will he ever be the same again?"[37] Fortunately for the nation, the President recovered quickly and completely.

The question of public information about the President's health continues to be a touchy one. A few months after his accession to office in 1961, President John F. Kennedy suffered a recurrence of a wartime back injury during a tree-planting ceremony in Ottawa, Canada. He was treated by his personal physician, Dr. Janet Travell, but the injury gave him trouble during his state visit to Europe. News of the President's difficulty was withheld from the public until his return to the United States—an error in judgment which provoked much criticism and gave rise to rumors that the injury might be more serious than the press had been led to believe. Subsequently the President came down with a virus infection, but this time there was no delay in announcing the news and lines of communication were ostentatiously kept open. Reporters were able to interview Dr. Travell, whom previously they had not been allowed to question.

The whole episode angered many of the White House press corps who had served under other Presidents. Merriman Smith, a UPI correspondent since Roosevelt's time, expressed himself on the subject during an interview by the author in Washington on July 1, 1961.

I think we were spoiled by the way in which Eisenhower handled the press during his illnesses. All of us around here got our degrees as doctors during that period. We read everything we could on heart trouble and when we questioned Dr. White we knew what he was talking about when he answered in medical terms. So we were irritated when we weren't informed about Kennedy's illness until a week after it had happened. Dr. Travell had her interview with us only after repeated requests and even then she wasn't altogether responsive.

Smith said that he had checked to see if it could be medically determined whether or not there was a connection between the back ailment and the virus infection, and had found that the only way was by means of a spinal tap and certain blood tests. He asked if such tests had been made and if so, what the results showed. According to Smith, Dr. Travell would state only that there was no connection between the two illnesses; she declined to be more specific.

There is no ground for believing that President Kennedy's ailment was anything other than it was represented to be, but the incident reminds us that what the public is told of a Chief Executive's health is still entirely up to the President himself or to the members of the palace guard.

Woodrow Wilson was a vigorous fifty-six when he entered on his first term of office. But the responsibilities of leadership in wartime increased the burden of the Presidency immeasurably, and his health had begun to suffer by the middle of his second term.

Culver

Wilson's illness—the most protracted instance of presidential disability in our history—ended his dream of United States participation in the League of Nations. He lived to finish out his term, but he left office on March 4, 1921, a disappointed and embittered man.

Wide World

On March 4, 1935, after two years in office, President Franklin D. Roosevelt looked younger than his fifty-four years. The question of his health did not arise when he was renominated in 1936 and 1940, but it was the major campaign issue in 1944.

Acme

When this picture was taken in November, 1944, five months before his death, Roosevelt had just been re-elected for the fourth time. It is now known that his health had been a source of anxiety in White House circles since the preceding January.

Harris & Ewing

In October, 1952, General Dwight D. Eisenhower was winding up the campaign which put him in the White House. The entire free world now looked to the United States for leadership, and the powers and responsibilities of the Presidency had become almost inconceivable.

Wide World

On November 11, 1955, recovered from his September 25 heart attack, Eisenhower left Denver for Washington. Failing to secure action from Congress providing for future lapses in executive power, he made a personal agreement with Vice President Richard M. Nixon.

Associated Press Wirephoto

John F. Kennedy, the youngest man ever to be elected President of the United States, came into office before his forty-fourth birthday. He wisely followed the example of his predecessor, and entered into an agreement with Vice President Lyndon Johnson providing for temporary inability.

Harris & Ewing

Kennedy is shown here in January, 1962, at the end of his first year as President. In the early days of his administration, the White House press staff was severely criticized for withholding the news that he had aggravated a back injury during a tree-planting ceremony in Ottawa.

Wide World

Chapter V

The Stopgap

1. THE EISENHOWER–NIXON AGREEMENT

The efforts of the Eisenhower administration to secure action on the question of delegating authority during a President's temporary disability have been described by former Attorney General Herbert Brownell, Jr., in an article which appeared in the *Yale Law Journal*.[1]

The battle began in January, 1956, when the President returned from Denver after recovering from his heart attack. At this time he directed Attorney General Brownell to "institute a full legal study of the problems raised by temporary presidential inability. His purpose was to draft a plan to protect the country fully if a President were to become disabled at a time when immediate executive action was needed" (p. 196). Brownell found that several authors had discussed the problem, but only one, Ruth Silva, had devoted an entire book to the subject. Her doctoral dissertation, *Presidential Succession,* presented at the University of Michigan in 1951, brought together many forgotten or obscure facts on presidential illnesses and laid the groundwork for future studies. So it was natural that the Attorney General should enlist her aid.

Practical political considerations, however, caused a postponement of the project. Nineteen fifty-six was an election year, and "it was decided not to formulate such a plan during the presidential campaign, lest it become entangled in partisan politics" (p. 196). But after his re-election, the President again went ahead with his campaign for the adoption of a practical law.

Early in January 1957, [he] reviewed several alternative plans and authorized the Attorney General to consult several persons outside the Government to obtain their views and criticisms. The opinion of members of the Cabinet were sought at a Cabinet meeting. Finally, a definitive plan which proposed a constitutional amendment was approved by the President. It was to be sent to the Congress with a special message from the President urging its adoption (p. 196).

But again, practical politics intervened. When the plan was presented at a meeting of congressional leaders of both parties, the Speaker of the House of Representatives, the late Sam Rayburn,

raised the point that if the President should send a special message to Congress urging the adoption of the proposed constitutional amendment, the people of the country, in the mistaken belief that some unannounced development in the President's condition had occurred, might become alarmed. Accordingly, the forthcoming special message was cancelled, and public announcement of the plan took the form of testimony by the Attorney General before a subcommittee of the Judiciary Committee of the House of Representatives (p. 196).

Brownell was given the fullest opportunity to explain the program, which was embodied in a proposed constitutional amendment. The operative clauses of the proposed amendment were as follows:

Section 1. In case of the removal of the President from office, or of his death or resignation, the Vice President shall become President for the unexpired portion of the then current term.

Section 2. If the President shall declare in writing that he is unable to discharge the powers and duties of his office, such powers and duties shall be discharged by the Vice President as Acting President.

Section 3. If the President does not so declare, the Vice President, if satisfied of the President's inability, and upon approval in writing of a majority of the heads of executive departments who are members of the President's Cabinet, shall discharge the powers and duties of Acting President.

Section 4. Whenever the President declares in writing that his inability is terminated, the President shall forthwith discharge the powers and duties of his office (p. 197).

At the time Brownell testified before the committee, several proposals already had been submitted, reflecting a variety of opinions. Congressman Peter J. Frelinghuysen (New

Jersey) thought the Supreme Court should decide a President's inability; Joseph C. O'Mahoney (Wyoming) contended that it should be determined by Congress; and Kenneth Keating (New York) was convinced that the whole matter should be adjudicated by a commission made up of congressional leaders, the Justices of the Supreme Court, and selected Cabinet members.

In ruling out these ideas, the Attorney General used a fundamental doctrine of constitutional law—the concept of separation of powers, which has developed in our law since the adoption of the Constitution. It states as a basic principle of our form of government that the executive, legislative, and judiciary branches must be kept separate from one another and free from the intrusions of the others into their respective domains. The President has invoked this doctrine to keep the files of the executive out of the hands of Congress; and the courts have used it to keep the lawmaking power of the President at a minimum.[2] In the present instance, it was the basis for Brownell's contention that the determination of presidential inability should be made within the executive branch; the President should not be subject to control and possible domination by either the Supreme Court or Congress. In this connection, the Attorney General read into the record a letter that Chief Justice Earl Warren had written to Representative Keating:

During the time the subject of inability of a President to discharge the duties of his office has been under discussion, the members of the Court have discussed generally . . . the proposal that a member or members of the Court be included in the membership of a Commission to determine the fact of Presidential inability to act.

It has been the belief of all of us that because of the separation of powers in our Government, the nature of the judicial process, the possibility of a controversy of this character coming to Court, and the danger of disqualification which might result in lack of a quorum, it would be inadvisable for any member of the Court to serve on such a commission.

. . . I do believe that the reasons above mentioned for nonparticipation of the Court are insurmountable.[3]

Brownell used a similar argument in repudiating the idea that Congress should decide the question.

With the participation of congressional officials a presidential inability commission would be bound to assume a political appearance. Individual members of Congress, though elected by the people, are elected by the people of a particular small district or state, and are not necessarily representative of the nation as a whole; only the President and the Vice President are elected by the entire populace.[4]

Before Brownell finished his testimony, the chairman of the committee, Representative Emanuel Celler of New York, and Representative William McCulloch of Ohio called attention to a serious gap in the administration's proposal. What happened, they wanted to know, if a President refused to give up his office, or if a President prematurely declared his recovery? They had in mind the case of a mentally disturbed Chief Executive who might develop an irrational hostility or a mistaken belief in his own fitness, or who was just plain stubborn and would not relinquish the post.* The Attorney General's answer was that a mentally ill or stubborn President could be impeached. But he was not entirely satisfied with this solution. As he later wrote:

. . . in the presentation of President Eisenhower's original proposal for a constitutional amendment in 1957, it was stated that any dispute between the President and the Vice

---

*"Suppose some President shall become insane immediately after his inauguration and shall remain so for two or three years. Will it then become the duty of the Vice-President to perform the functions of the Presidential office? Clearly it will. Then, while the insanity continues, will the Vice-President be President or still only Vice-President? Surely the latter, for the President is still alive, and is, consequently, still the holder of the office. His title to it can only end by his removal, death or resignation. He cannot be removed pending his insanity except on conviction of treason, bribery or other high crimes and misdemeanors. He has not resigned, and an attempted resignation would be a nullity. If the Vice-President remains Vice-President under these conditions, how can he be else in case of the death of the President? The office or its powers and duties 'devolve' on him as fully in one case as in the other" (Lewis R. Works, "The Succession of the Vice-President under the Constitution—An Interrogation," *American Law Review*, XXXVIII [1904], 501).

President regarding termination of the President's disability could be resolved by Congress's taking impeachment proceedings against whichever official was wrongfully attempting to exercise the powers of the presidency. In subsequent public discussion of the proposal, however, it was pointed out that impeachment and trial are complicated and lengthy processes, that the Congress is not always in session, and that nothing in the Constitution now empowers the Vice President to call Congress into special session. Furthermore, conviction would remove the President permanently, and the odium attached to the impeachment might very well cause many Congressmen to hesitate to take such action—especially against an ill man.[5]

Representatives Celler and McCulloch also questioned the wisdom of the Vice President's consulting with the Cabinet before assuming office as acting President: the Cabinet, after all, is composed of political appointees who owe their political lives to the incumbent President. In countering this argument, Brownell cited the Tyler precedent as the reason the Garfield and Wilson Cabinets did not call in the Vice President. Thus, he reflected Silva's view that it was the fear the Vice President would oust the President that kept Arthur and Marshall from becoming acting Presidents.* And this was only half true.

At the conclusion of the hearings, the Attorney General's proposal went by the board. No legislator pretended to have the answers to the problems of presidential disability, but there was a feeling that something basic was lacking in all the legislation considered, and the subcommittee refused to

---

*The Attorney General's testimony indicates that he was placing heavy reliance on Silva's research. See *Hearings, Special Subcommittee on Presidential Disability of the Judiciary Committee, House*, 85th Cong., 1st Sess., p. 14. Other congressional hearings were held in 1956 and 1958. (*Hearings, Special Committee to Study Presidential Inability, Committee on the Judiciary, House*, 84th Cong., 2nd Sess., April 11, 12, 1956; *Hearings, Subcommittee on Constitutional Amendments, Committee on the Judiciary, Senate*, 85th Cong., 2nd Sess., January 24, February 11, 14, 18 and 28, 1958). The House Committee of the 84th Congress prepared and sent out a questionnaire which was published with the replies as a Committee Print, January 31, 1956; an analysis was published March 26, 1957.

recommend any one approach. Sherman Adams notes that at the very beginning of the venture Senator Knowland voiced the opposition to the Cabinet's being involved in questions of determining inability. Knowland also brought up the problem of a mentally ill President who would not give up the office, or who would try to resume it before he was fully recovered. At this early stage, no attempt had been made to compromise, and, as Adams writes: "There being no unanimity and little enthusiasm among the Republican leaders and strong opposition from Rayburn, it was apparent that the proposal would not get far. . . ."[6]

The criticism of the impeachment process as a method of resolving a dispute between the President and the Vice President over the former's recovery continued after Congress had adjourned. In response to these criticisms the new Attorney General, William P. Rogers, on February 18, 1958, presented a revised Section 4 for the proposed amendment:

Whenever the President declares in writing that his inability has terminated, the President shall forthwith discharge the powers and duties of his office: *Provided, however,* that if the Vice President and a majority of the heads of executive departments who are members of the President's Cabinet shall signify in writing that the President's inability has not been terminated thereupon:

(*a*) The Congress shall forthwith consider the issue of the President's inability in accordance with procedures provided for impeachment, and if the Congress is not in session, shall forthwith convene for this purpose;

(*b*) If the House of Representatives shall on record vote charge that the President's inability has not terminated, and the Senate so finds by the concurrence of two thirds of the members present, the powers and duties of the office of President shall be discharged by the Vice President as Acting President for the remainder of the term, or until Congress by a majority vote of the members of both Houses determines that the President's inability has terminated.[7]

This proposal also failed for lack of support, as did a similar bill backed by a bipartisan group led by Senators Kefauver of Tennessee and Hruska of Nebraska.

It was against this background of congressional inaction that President Eisenhower, on March 3, 1958, entered into a private agreement with Vice President Richard Nixon which would enable Nixon to act as President if circumstances required. Eisenhower had discussed the problem with Nixon a number of times since his heart attack. In these discussions, according to Nixon, the President

had mentioned several alternatives, but kept coming back to the idea of a letter which would give the Vice President alone the authority to decide when the President was unable to carry on—that is, when the President himself was unable to make the decision.

In early February, the President called Rogers and me into his office, commented that he thought he had licked the problem, and handed each of us a copy of a letter. . . . We made some minor suggestions and he incorporated them into the letter and then sent it on to his secretary, Ann Whitman, for final typing. Marked PERSONAL AND SECRET, one copy went to me, one to Bill Rogers as Attorney General, and one to John Foster Dulles, as Secretary of State and ranking member of the Cabinet.

With the exception of our very minor suggestions, the letter was wholly Eisenhower's in concept and drafting, and it was a masterpiece. Leaving the White House, Bill Rogers remarked that Eisenhower would have made an outstanding lawyer, for the letter handled the contingencies of a very complex problem from every angle and was as good a drafting job as any constitutional expert could have done.[8]

The terms of this letter, which reduced to a memorandum the President's and Vice President's understanding of the constitutional role of the Vice President as Acting President, were made public on March 3, 1958. They are as follows:

The President and the Vice President have agreed that the following procedures are in accord with the purposes and provisions of Article 2, Section 1, of the Constitution, dealing with Presidential inability. They believe that these procedures, which are intended to apply to themselves only, are in no sense outside or contrary to the Constitution but are consistent with its present provisions and implement its clear intent.

1. In the event of inability the President would—if possible—so inform the Vice President, and the Vice President would serve as Acting President, exercising the powers and duties of the office until the inability had ended.

2. In the event of an inability which would prevent the President from so communicating with the Vice President, the Vice President, after such consultation as seems to him appropriate under the circumstances, would decide upon the devolution of the powers and duties of the Office and would serve as Acting President until the inability had ended.

3. The President, in either event, would determine when the inability had ended and at that time would resumé the full exercise of the powers and duties of the Office.[9]

Commenting on this memorandum in his *Yale Law Journal* article (which appeared some eight months after the historic agreement was made public), Herbert Brownell wrote that it

represents the Eisenhower Administration's interpretation of the Constitution as it now stands. The only addition to present Constitutional requirements is that the Vice President take action "after such consultation as seems to him appropriate under the circumstances." Although the Constitution does not require the Vice President to consult anyone, it was felt that, as a matter of good judgment, the Vice President would want to consult members of the Cabinet, congressional leaders of both parties, and perhaps other prominent citizens before presuming to exercise the powers and duties of the presidency. The Eisenhower-Nixon understanding, in effect, gives the Vice President the comfort of being directed to seek opinion from other persons and thus strengthen his position if he should be obliged to take these steps. Appropriately, in view of constitutional silence on the matter, the persons with whom the Vice President is to consult are not mentioned. Presumably, the Vice President's choice would depend on the circumstances of the moment; in time of international crisis the opportunity for consultation might be very brief.[10]

Thus, Eisenhower became the first President in our history to take cognizance of and act upon a serious defect in our Constitution. But the agreement was a purely personal one between Eisenhower and Nixon, and could not, therefore, apply to their successors. President John F. Kennedy, when he succeeded to office, did enter into a similar agreement with Vice President Lyndon Johnson, but, as former Vice President Nixon points out,

. . . the agreement President Eisenhower set forth in his letter to me, and the one President Kennedy has entered into with Vice President Johnson, are only as good as the will of the parties to keep them. Presidents and Vice Presidents have not always had the mutual trust and cordial relations President Eisenhower had with me or that President Kennedy has had with Vice President Johnson up to this time. Jealousies and rivalries can develop within an Administration which could completely destroy such an agreement.

Only a constitutional amendment can solve the problem on a permanent basis. President Eisenhower's agreement with me was personal and had the force of authority only during his term of office. President Kennedy's agreement is similarly limited. These agreements, which are mere expressions of a President's desires, do not have the force of law. Even a law passed by Congress might be subject to constitutional challenge. However, such a law would express the will of Congress and should be passed while the incumbent President is in good health and before a presidential election year drags politics into an already complex problem. The experiences of Garfield, Wilson, and Eisenhower should have taught us a lesson. Surely the time has come for a truly bipartisan program to draw up a constitutional amendment which would define the rights and duties of a Vice President during any period when the President of the United States is incapacitated.

The urgent need for such an amendment becomes crystal clear when a President is disabled, but that is precisely the time when politics bar any reasonable agreement on the wording of such an amendment. . . . It is hardly necessary to point out that these perilous times in which we live will continue, and more than ever before our nation will need an able and healthy Chief Executive or acting Chief Executive at all times. . . .

The heart attack, the ileitis operation, and the stroke were . . . potential constitutional crises of the greatest magnitude for the nation. If such a crisis should arise in the future its outcome should not be dependent upon the personal whims of whoever happens to hold the offices of President and Vice President, but on the law of the land, as approved by the Congress or set forth in the Constitution.[11]

2. THE KENNEDY–JOHNSON AGREEMENT

In December, 1960, President-elect Kennedy and Vice President-elect Johnson made a tentative informal agreement, similar to that which had existed between Eisenhower and Nixon, on the procedures to be followed should Kennedy become disabled. Soon after the new administration took office, the President asked Attorney General Robert F. Kennedy for an opinion on the construction to be given the presidential inability clause of the Constitution. Specifically, President Kennedy wanted to know:

first, whether when presidential inability occurs, the Vice President . . . succeeds to the "Office," *i.e.*, becomes President and remains in the office even if the inability should cease; second, who determines whether the inability exists and who determines whether the inability has ended; and third, whether the memorandum of March 3, 1958, between former President Eisenhower and former Vice President Nixon . . . is a desirable precedent for this administration to follow.[12]

Assistant Attorney General Nicholas deB. Katzenbach, Robert Kennedy's legal adviser, was assigned to review the problem and subsequently drafted the opinion which was delivered to the President on August 2, 1961. In summarizing his conclusions, the Attorney General stated:

In my judgment, there is no question that the Vice President acts as President in the event of the President's inability and acts in that capacity "until the disability be removed." . . .
I believe also that there is no substantial question that it is the Vice President, if the President is unable to do so, who determines the President's inability and that it is the President who asserts when the inability has ceased. These conclusions are supported by the great majority of reputable scholars who have examined the problem, as well as by my predecessors. . . .

I am of the opinion that the understanding between the President and the Vice President . . . is clearly constitutional and as close to spelling out a practical solution to the problem as is possible.[13]

In the discussion preceding this summary, the Attorney General had noted that since the Eisenhower-Nixon understanding

may prove to be a persuasive precedent of what the Constitution means until it is amended or other action is taken, I would favor that the Administration follow it. Cumulative precedents of this kind may be valuable in the future.[14]

On August 10, 1961, President Kennedy announced adoption of the Eisenhower precedent, and a summary of the provisions of the agreement, identical with that of the Eisenhower-Nixon understanding, was made public in a press release the same day.

There already are two schools of legal thought concerning this memorandum: one group (which does not include Eisenhower or Kennedy) regards it as a perfect solution to the problem and sees no need for further action; at the other extreme are those who hold that it is unconstitutional. Not only because of this divergence of opinion but because an examination of the specific provisions may help to bring into focus the real problems of disability, a closer scrutiny of the agreement is indicated.

Without congressional action, a memorandum is the only way a President can set up a formal procedure to cover inability. But a memorandum is discretionary with each new administration, and this, of course, is one of the chief drawbacks of the inability agreement. A President who wishes to ignore the memorandum may do so. He may also adopt a completely different formula for making the determination. In either case the net result would be even greater uncertainty than now exists.

Section 1 states that a disabled President would, if possible, inform the Vice President of his condition, in which case the Vice President would take over as Acting President until the inability is ended. Because it allows a President to step down temporarily, this provision—in the view of Attorneys General Brownell and Kennedy—serves to negate the Tyler precedent; and—so they reason—if the Tyler precedent is nullified, a disabled President will not hesitate to give up his job. He is assured of resuming it upon his recovery. The provision is based on Silva's assumption that Garfield's and Wilson's refusal to step aside derived from the Tyler precedent. But such an assumption is a gross oversimplification of a complex problem. John Tyler's decision offered a comfortable and plausible excuse for the failure to call in Arthur and Marshall; in neither case did it motivate the refusal.

General Eisenhower, in discussing the memorandum with the author, particularly stressed that its strength depends entirely upon the good will existing between the President and the Vice President.[15] He must have had in mind the historical evidence that there was no good will between Garfield and Arthur and only a semblance of it between Wilson and Marshall. The point is that we have not changed our system of choosing the President and Vice President; political expediency can still determine a ticket; and politics makes strange bedfellows. The possibility of a rift between the incumbents should neither be overlooked nor minimized, and there is no protection against such an eventuality in the present memorandum.

While it is certainly wise to allow a President who wishes to do so to step aside, the question history poses is not *should* he? or *can* he? but *will* he? Whether we like it or not, no President, if we are to judge by past performances, is likely to give up his office—to relinquish it voluntarily to a subordinate.

When President Eisenhower announced that he would run for a second term, he promised the American people that he would resign from the Presidency if his health should fail.* The resignation of the President would have

---

* "I have said unless I felt absolutely up to the performance of the duties of the President, the second that I didn't, I would no longer be there in the job or I wouldn't be available for the job."—President Eisenhower in a press conference, March 7, 1956. Quoted in Nixon, *Six Crises*, p. 176.

been unprecedented in the nation's history. The only re-
motely analogous situation occurred in 1832 when John C.
Calhoun resigned the Vice Presidency, and his action was
in no way connected with his health. He split with President Andrew Jackson over the issue of state rights. The
agricultural states of the South were burdened with what
they called the "Tariff of Abominations," a protective levy
which, so the Southerners said, favored the manufacturers of
the North at the expense of the plantation owners. Calhoun,
a South Carolinian, wrote a stirring essay setting forth the
doctrine that no state could be bound by a federal law
which it regarded as unconstitutional. Since President Jackson stood for a strong central government, a deep rift developed between him and the Vice President, and Calhoun
ultimately resigned to enter the Senate, where he became
the leading proponent of state rights. Although Presidents
and Vice Presidents have had differences approaching feuds,
none except Calhoun has ever resigned for any cause.

Reluctance to surrender power is a very human charac-
teristic, and the man who is President of the United States
is the most powerful man in the modern world. Moreover,
there is no position more calculated to build a man's ego.
Edward R. Murrow describes the White House as being "a
kind of alchemist. There little men have grown great, and
great men have become giants."[16] To complete the picture
he should have added—"and all but a very few have become
indispensable to the nation—in their own minds."

Until 1940, the two-term tradition initiated by George
Washington was unwritten law. Except for those Presidents
who died during their first term or were not renominated,
how many between Washington and Franklin D. Roosevelt
gave up the office after only one term? James K. Polk took
office in 1845 with "the settled purpose of not being a candidate for re-election"; Rutherford B. Hayes made it known
early in 1876 that he would not run again "under any circumstances." That makes two, and Calvin Coolidge might
be counted as a third, depending on whether one puts the
emphasis on *I* or *choose* in his statement "I do not choose
to run." Four Presidents—William Henry Harrison, Zachary
Taylor, Garfield, and Harding—died during their first term.

Five—Tyler, Pierce, Buchanan, Johnson, and Arthur—were not renominated. Excluding Washington, who founded the tradition, and the nine Presidents who died or were not renominated, only three out of the remaining twenty vacated the White House before tradition compelled them to do so.

The force of the White House as an ego-builder can also be seen in more recent history. The circumstances surrounding Franklin D. Roosevelt's decision to run for a third term have been described fully by James A. Farley, Judge Samuel Rosenman, and others. The President had given Farley and Secretary of State Hull reason to believe that he would support them to head the Democratic ticket in 1940. But with the war crisis coming on—and even though the Republican nominee, Wendell Willkie, was no isolationist and, in fact, helped to create the bipartisan foreign policy of World War II—Roosevelt decided that his experience was indispensable to the proper handling of the situation. This indispensable man was the same F.D.R. who said in 1932, "The genius of America is greater than any candidate or any party." And it was the same F.D.R. for whom Rosenman helped prepare the speech given at Shibe Park in Philadelphia on October 27, 1944. Rosenman says about that address:

> Roosevelt wanted to talk about the strenuous and exacting role a President has to carry as Commander-in-Chief of the Army and Navy in the conduct of a war. The political point was obvious even though unspoken: That the man who since 1937 had been preparing the country physically and mentally for what was coming, who had been conducting a successful global war for almost four years, should be continued in office to finish the job; that it would be inadvisable to turn it over to inexperienced hands.[17]

Josephus Daniels, Secretary of the Navy under Woodrow Wilson, has set down some pungent comments on the prevailing desire of our Chief Executives to prolong their White House tenancy, though not all of them were as insistent as Roosevelt upon their indispensability.

> Why do I think Wilson, even though partially paralyzed, would have felt constrained to have accepted if nominated? Because he would have regarded it as a command with a vital principle as the issue, and his views were so well known

that personal campaigning would not be necessary. There is another reason based upon some acquaintance with Presidents and some knowledge of politics and history. It is my deliberate judgment that, since Andrew Jackson returned to the Hermitage after having hand-picked Martin Van Buren as his successor and paved the way for Polk, his political protégé, to carry on his policies—since Old Hickory's day, no President has willingly left the White House. There is something about the office and place that makes all after-life lack that something which only the White House gives. If Wilson had been a well man, he would, in my opinion, have been willing to break the old three-term jinx in devotion to the League. It is well known that Theodore Roosevelt expected to resume residence after one term for Taft, and that he never lost the *animus revertandi*, even bolting the Republican Party in 1912 and organizing a new party which he thought would lead to the White House. Most people believe if he had lived he would have been given the Republican nomination in 1920. When Cleveland's term expired in 1889, he declared that he was happy to be relieved of the duties and retire to private life. But he was fooling himself and the public, he did not fool his wife. As she was leaving the White House she told a faithful Negro who had long been there, "Keep everything as it is now so that we will find no change when we return in 1893."

Taft felt that Teddy had "done him wrong" when he sought to oust him in 1912 but was somewhat consoled when he was made Chief Justice. He wanted a second term and felt he was entitled to such an encore when Wilson won. When Coolidge said "I do not choose to run," he thought that delphic utterance would cause the people to break the third-term tradition for him without his initiating it. No man was ever more disappointed when his statement was construed to mean that he did not desire the nomination.

Hoover has never really found himself since his ejection from the White House. No President ever worked harder than Hoover, or, in his own peculiar way, enjoyed being President more than Hoover. It was not his fault that the depression came to make his reelection impossible.

Franklin Roosevelt loved the great office to which he added distinction. He did not need great persuasion to accept nominations that gave him the unprecedented honor of being elected four times.[18]

After four years at the head of the mightiest nation in the world a man is bound to feel indispensable. It is a natural reaction to the adulation the President receives from the public, and to the customs which have attached to the presidency. From the minute he occupies the national shrine called the White House a President is constantly reminded of his importance. "Ladies first" does not apply at the White House—protocol demands that the President get into the car first; when the President enters a room, everyone stands; no one leaves a room before he does; the President is served first at all meals; wherever he appears he is the center of interest, attention, solicitude—"Hail to the Chief!" blare all the bands. No law can change the deeply rooted tendency toward presidential deification. Since prehistoric times human beings have stood in awe of power, and a President is a symbol of power. Homage to the President is often justified on the grounds that it is paid to the office, not the officeholder, but it cannot fail to affect him: a man who has experienced the pomp and circumstance of the presidency can never again be as other men.

George Washington, who observed the weaknesses of men in times of triumph as well as of trial, wisely set the two-term tradition. When that precedent was finally broken by Franklin Roosevelt, the American people, much as they revered F.D.R., amended the Constitution to make it certain that no President ever again would hold office longer than eight years. But the people, by their adulation of the President, share the responsibility for the "indispensable President" concept, whether it is in connection with the two-term tradition or with presidential inability. It was fitting that we should limit the term of office; it is equally appropriate for us to stifle the misguided ambition of a sick executive and insist that he surrender his powers until he is well. Therefore, while the Kennedy-Johnson memorandum wisely allows a President to step aside temporarily, the history of the Presidency and human nature, not the Tyler precedent, make it highly unlikely that he will do so.

Section 2 of the presidential memorandum provides for a situation in which the President is unable to communicate with the Vice President. If such a situation should arise the Vice President may take action "after such consultation as seems to him appropriate under the circumstances."

All those who have undertaken studies of any depth agree that, under the present Constitution, the Vice President determines disability. It is inconceivable that the delegates to the Constitutional Convention, with their practical approach to these matters, intended the Vice President to make the decision without ascertaining the facts of the President's illness. To do this adequately, he would first have to consult with the President's doctors, then the Cabinet. If time allowed, he might also wish to discuss the matter with the President's family. So, when the memorandum allows the Vice President such "consultation as seems to him appropriate under the circumstances," it is merely reflecting the present state of the Constitution. Of course, if consultation were required with specific people, this would amount to amending the Constitution by memorandum. Such a result would follow any understanding that a certain person, say the Attorney General, were to be consulted.

This section, as it presently stands, may be good constitutional law, but here again the law is far removed from practicality. Was Thomas R. Marshall kept informed of Wilson's condition? Well enough informed to make a decision on disability? Was Arthur carefully advised of Garfield's progress during the eighty days the President was disabled? The basic problem is one of keeping the Vice President *and the public* informed. The public announcements during the Eisenhower illnesses were as novel as they were appropriate, and it must not be forgotten that they were entirely discretionary on the part of the President and his official family. There is no assurance that future Presidents will follow the Eisenhower precedent rather than the practices of Garfield and Wilson. There is no law in 1962 which even requires the President to have a physical examination, let alone make the results public; any President may refuse to tell anyone anything about the state of his health. "Why not?" say some people. "It's a private matter." Such reasoning gives inordinate emphasis to the right of privacy, a right which any man who enters public life relinquishes in part. The health of the President of the United States in the twentieth century is not only every American's business, it is also of vital importance to millions of foreign peoples.

Section 3 of the agreement states that whether the President or the Vice President has declared the inability, the President may determine when it is over, and forthwith resume the full exercise of the powers and duties of the office. Since it was this proviso in the original Eisenhower program which drew fire from Congress, and which was amended in the subsequent proposal to provide for the removal of an unwilling President without impeachment, it is surprising to find Attorney General Robert Kennedy's opinion ignoring this aspect of the situation. While he cites Rogers and Brownell in support of the idea that the President should determine his own recovery, he omits any reference to the fact that Eisenhower, Brownell, and Rogers all subsequently agreed on the necessity for changing their proposed constitutional amendment. The Attorney General *cites no other authorities* in this regard, and ends the argument by quoting the remarks made by Senator Cole in 1881 that the remedy should be by impeachment.

The opinion and the memorandum are subject to valid criticism on another point. Attorney General Kennedy stresses throughout his opinion that it is the Vice President who determines disability. But this power carries with it the implication that the Vice President also determines when there is no disability, in other words, when he should *not* act as President. Thus, the Attorney General's reasoning is illogical, for if the Vice President does not determine when the President is well, how is he supposed to determine when he is ailing? Before the Attorney General's reasoning in this respect is accepted, he will have to produce considerably more authority to make absolutely certain that a shift in vested constitutional powers is not being accomplished by a private memorandum.

There are several drawbacks to the alternate procedure of having the Congress determine the President's recovery if there is a dispute. First of all, such a procedure is illogical.

Although its proponents, Rogers and Brownell, did not favor letting Congress determine disability when the President first takes ill, when a dispute arises between a President and the Vice President later on, they suggest that the matter be resolved by a two-thirds vote of both Houses. Why is it a violation of the separation of powers doctrine in one instance and not in the other? The same reasons which militate against Congress deciding the problem in the first place are even more applicable when the two executives differ. A prompt decision would be required and congressional determination would take months—and how many congressmen could resist the opportunity to make political capital out of the situation?

The imperfections and potential trouble spots in the memorandum should be apparent. Both Eisenhower and Kennedy recognize the need for Congressional action. It will take much more than a private understanding to insure perpetuation of the wise precedent established by President Eisenhower.

This was amply proven by the fact that Congress has made no provision for the publication or even the preservation of the originals of the Eisenhower-Nixon and Kennedy-Johnson agreements. There is no provision for depositing the original Eisenhower memorandum with the Secretary of State or publishing it in the *Federal Register*. According to Ann Whitman, it was necessary for the Eisenhower-Nixon agreement to be "very tightly held and to my certain knowledge less than a handful of people in Washington have ever seen the documents."[19] The same situation prevails with regard to the Kennedy-Johnson agreement. It is only by the grace of the two Presidents that these private understandings were made public. Almost any type of arrangement could be made on this crucial subject, and there exists no legal requirement that it be made public. It is a strange situation when the law requires publication of presidential proclamations on matters involving the administration of Palmyra Island, National Forest Products Week, and delegation of authority with respect to foreign assistance,[20] but an agreement determining succession to the presidency must be "tightly held"!

Chapter VI

Colonial Precedents and State Laws

Every attempt to find a solution to the problems of presidential inability must begin with the Constitution itself—with a study not only of the succession clause and of other provisions, but of the records and history of the Constitutional Convention, the debates in the Convention and the ratifying conventions, and also such contemporary writings as Madison's *Notes* and Hamilton's *Federalist* papers.

All previous scholars, however, have confined themselves to the proceedings of the Federal Convention, and the degree to which the presidential inability clause is based on similar clauses in colonial charters and state constitutions has never been thoroughly considered.* Yet since precedent and personal experience are great opinion-molders, these documents surely merit examination. As Attorney General Robert F. Kennedy has written:

> In attempting to ascertain the intention of the framers of the Constitution, it is helpful to know what the practice was in the thirteen States when the Constitution was adopted. We would expect that the provisions of those State Constitutions dealing with succession in event of a governor's inability definitely influenced and shaped the thinking of the framers of the Constitution in determining what provisions should be made in event of presidential inability. Accordingly we may consider those State constitutional provisions as a guide in interpreting the corresponding succession clause in the Constitution of the United States.[1]

1. COLONIAL PRECEDENTS

The pre-Federal period (1604–1789) affords many examples of a "deputie governour" temporarily performing the governor's duties. The conditions of frontier life made such

---

*The notable exception is Irving Williams, *The Rise of the Vice Presidency* (New York: Public Affairs Press, 1956), where colonial experience is considered with reference to secondary sources (p. 16).

forehanded arrangements essential if there were not to be lapses in executive power. Traveling involved months, not hours. Common disasters were not atomic in nature, but common disasters there were. Danger to the community as a whole was always imminent—from the Indians, from epidemic disease. A measure of the colonists' chances for survival is tellingly expressed in a single statistic: during this period the average life span for males was twenty-seven years.

The uncertainties of existence in the New World were certainly borne in mind by the delegates to the Constitutional Convention. Many of the delegates were lawyers and thoroughly conversant with the provisions in colonial charters framed for the specific purpose of preventing voids in the exercise of power. Colonial practice in this respect remained virtually the same from founding of the first colony, Jamestown, until the adoption of the Constitution.

A deputy governor for Jamestown was named as early as 1617, three years after the colony was founded. Moreover, due to the chief executive's inability to depart for his post, the deputy governor was obliged to assume office.[2]

William Penn received the grant of Pennsylvania from King Charles II in 1681; he was resident in the colony from 1682 to 1684, and then returned to England. The King's grant refers to the "governor, or his Deputy," but says nothing about the procedure required for the deputy to assume office. In 1689 it was necessary for Penn, then Governor of Pennsylvania, to report to the King on the status of the colony. He wrote to the Pennsylvania Assembly:

And if you Desire a Deputy Governor rather, name three, or five, and I shall name one of them, so as you Consider of a Comfortable substance, that ye Government may not go a begging.[3]

Penn thereafter appointed a man as deputy and lieutenant to act in his name.

Seventeen of the colonial charters and constitutions in effect at various times before the adoption of the Federal Constitution provide for a lieutenant governor or his equivalent. Fifteen of the seventeen gave him status as "acting governor"; and of the fifteen, four provide for the governor's powers to be exercised during his absence, ten for the inability or "sickness" of the governor. Colonial precedent is clear. Only the constitutions of South Carolina of 1776 and 1777 state that the lieutenant governor *succeeds* to the office of governor, and these provisions were later amended. In April, 1961, the constitutions of eleven of the original thirteen states adhered to colonial practice. Only Rhode Island and Virginia follow the "Tyler trend."[4]

The very early charters of the colonies gave the governing power to the owners or their descendants. If an owner was absent, his son could assume his powers and there would be no delay in the execution of the laws. The same rule applied when a governor died. In cases of inability, the governor "deputized" the lieutenant governor, otherwise the latter automatically made the determination. This custom of automatic transfer of power developed at the same time as the rule of descent. In line with the latter concept, some of the charters provided for a regency if the owner's descendant was a minor.* But as democracy evolved in the colonies, deputization replaced succession by descent as the general practice, and this custom continued after the Declaration of Independence.

Alexander Hamilton refers to state disability provisions in *The Federalist*. After discussing the Federal Convention's reasons for electing a Vice President and making him presiding officer of the Senate, Hamilton says:

. . . The other consideration is, that as the Vice President may occasionally become a *substitute* for the President, in the supreme executive magistracy, all the reasons which recommend the mode of election prescribed for the one, apply with great if not with equal force to the manner of appointing the other. It is remarkable that in this, as in most other instances, the objection which is made would lie against the constitution of this state [New York]. We have a Lieutenant-Governor, chosen by the people at large, who presides in the Senate, and is the constitutional substitute for

*The disability provisions of all the colonial charters and early state constitutions may be found in Appendix II.

the Governor, in casualties *similar* to those which would authorize the Vice-President to exercise and discharge the duties of the President.[5]

Thus, the spirit and the letter of the law of the pre-Federal period substantiates the interpretation placed on the inability clause of the Federal Constitution by Henry E. Davis at the time of President Garfield's illness, and by a majority of scholars since that date, including Eisenhower's and Kennedy's Attorneys General.

2. EXPERIENCE IN THE STATES SINCE 1789

Obviously the interpretation given a state constitution cannot be applied to the federal document, except by comparison. But we have had four or five times as many governors as Presidents, and there is a correspondingly greater amount of experience from which to draw in appraising laws of succession.

Disability clauses in state constitutions, as in the Federal Constitution, are part of a general section dealing with succession. Disability is grouped with other contingencies, like impeachment or death. In order to understand the interpretation given to the disability clause of the succession section, it is necessary to examine the cases dealing with the other contingencies.

Death

The question of succession in the states most frequently follows the death of the chief executive. It becomes a court matter, as a rule, when the man who has to fill the governor's shoes wants to know if he will receive the governor's salary.

The first interpretation of a succession clause dates back to the death of Governor DeWitt Clinton of New York, who died on February 11, 1828. Nathaniel Pritcher, Lieutenant Governor, raised the question of whether he was entitled to the salary of governor or lieutenant governor. William M. Marcy, comptroller of New York, said Pritcher was *acting* governor, and entitled by law to the salary given the governor.

The state courts have followed Marcy's ruling in "succession by death" cases, right up to the most recent one in Florida in 1953.[6] The only exceptions have been in Oregon and Wyoming.[7] In Wyoming, for example, the second man in line is the secretary of state, a common line of succession in smaller states which find eliminating a paycheck for lieutenant governor a convenient method of economizing. But the Wyoming court seemed not to be thinking of economy when it ruled that the secretary of state, when he acts as governor, is entitled to *both* salaries. This is an odd decision for any state to make and certainly places Wyoming in a class by itself.

There is no question that a majority of state courts, in these "succession by death" cases, have refused to follow the Tyler precedent.

Impeachment

Succession by impeachment is a completely different type of situation from succession by death. The word "impeachment" itself is often misunderstood: it refers to the proceeding by which an executive is accused of wrongdoing and brought to trial. At the federal and state levels, the actual complaint is made by the House of Representatives, and the trial is held in the Senate, with the Chief Justice presiding. The senators act as the jury. The legal questions surrounding impeachment in the states involve the problem of whether the governor is suspended from his duties at the time of filing of the charges against him, or after his conviction. If he is suspended, what is the status of the person who acts as governor during the interval? The leading case originates in Nebraska.

In the early 1870's Nebraska had a young Republican governor, David Butler, who had overstepped the law in encouraging land sales and pushing the building of the state Capitol in the new town of Lincoln. The legislature had been inclined to excuse technical irregularities in appreciation of his great services to the public, but Butler continued to cut corners and play fast and loose, and a day of reckoning finally came. When the Governor was unable to account satisfactorily for funds collected from the sale of school lands, the house of representatives approved articles of impeachment against him and he was subsequently convicted on the charge that he had appropriated the funds collected from the federal government to his own use. At the time the articles of impeachment were filed, the legislature addressed a letter to the state supreme court asking its opinion regarding Butler's status pending his trial by the senate. Justices Lake and Crounse held that in the case of impeachment the functions of the governor are entirely suspended until his acquittal, when they again become operative, or until his conviction, when the suspension becomes permanent.[8] Butler was, of course, permanently removed from office, but the important aspect of the decision is that the secretary of state became *acting governor* during the proceedings against the chief executive. Similar holdings have been made in New York, North Dakota, and Oklahoma.[9] Thus, here again the Tyler trend has been disregarded and the precedent established from colonial times recognized and applied by the states.

Resignation

If governors are not as reluctant as Presidents to relinquish office, the answer no doubt resides in the relative importance of their posts: a governor, unlike a President, may be able to climb to a higher rung on the political ladder. At any rate, political advancement seems to be most frequently the motivating factor in gubernatorial resignations.

One case in which it did not figure occurred in 1829 when Sam Houston resigned as Governor of Tennessee because of a quarrel with his wife. He had unjustly accused her of infidelity, and Mrs. Houston—after verbally scalping the old Indian fighter—packed up and left. When no amount of pleading could induce her to return, Houston felt that his domestic difficulties might undermine public confidence in him. He wrote to his lieutenant governor:

. . . Although shielded by a perfect consciousness of undiminished claim to the confidence and support of my fellow citizens, yet delicately circumstanced as I am and by my own misfortunes, more than by the fault or contrivance of anyone, overwhelmed by sudden calamities, it is certainly

due to myself and respectful to the world, that I should retire from a position which, in the public judgment, I might
seem to occupy by questionable authority.[10]

In recent years a divorced man has twice been nominated
for the Presidency, and to us today Houston's statement
might seem overemotional and unnecessary, but his attitude
was wholly consistent with nineteenth-century morals.

Houston's case was unique. Most governors resign to
accept a federal appointment or to campaign for a higher
office. Martin Van Buren, for example, resigned as Governor
of New York to run for President. When the traditional
question arose as to the status of his successor, Lieutenant
Governor Enos T. Throop, the question was decided by
Silas Wright, then comptroller, in the same manner as his
predecessor had decided the Clinton-Pritcher case. Wright
said that Throop became acting governor, exercising the
powers and duties of the office.[11]

Five other court cases are reported concerning governors
who resigned.[12] In four cases the men involved quit the
governorship to advance their political careers: Governors
Joseph T. Robinson of Kansas and Francis E. Warren of
Wyoming resigned to take office as United States Senators,
while Governor John W. Griggs of New Jersey became Attorney General of the United States. Governor James H.
Peabody of Colorado resigned in favor of his lieutenant
governor, but remained in the political spotlight and later
became United States Senator. There have been other cases
of gubernatorial resignations, but they did not come before
the courts. While figures are not available, the trend evidenced in the court cases would probably be followed.

In sharp contrast to those situations in which incumbents voluntarily abandon the governor's chair are the
dramas enacted when men are either so hellbent to attain
the office or to hang onto it that they will resort to force.
Governor-elect Eugene Talmadge of Georgia died on December 1, 1946, before publication by the legislature of the
returns verifying his election; M. E. Thompson was the
lieutenant governor-elect. The Talmadge machine had controlled Georgia politics for years, so it came as no surprise

when the legislature proceeded to name Herman Talmadge, son of the late Governor-elect, for the office. However, Georgia's laws provide that the legislature can select a governor only if the people fail to cast a majority of votes for one candidate. The Georgia Supreme Court, where the contest was taken, decided that Eugene Talmadge, though dead when the votes were counted, had received a majority, hence the legislators' choice of Herman Talmadge was void.[13] Then who *was* governor? Thompson? But he had been elected lieutenant governor. What about Ellis Arnall, the incumbent governor? The supreme court said Arnall held over as governor, not acting governor. On January 18, 1947, Arnall resigned in favor of Thompson. Herman Talmadge instantly declared war, establishing a beachhead on Arnall's doorstep when the latter refused to surrender to the machine, and only quick action by the supreme court made a peace treaty possible. The Georgia judges endorsed Thompson's right to the governor's chair, but—in a decision oddly at variance with their earlier ruling—said that Thompson was *acting governor*. The case illustrates what can happen when the law is fuzzy and men are greedy.

An even more fantastic game of Musical Chairs occurred in Louisiana in 1930 when Louisiana's "Kingfish"—Governor Huey P. Long—was elected to the United States Senate. Lieutenant Governor Paul Narcisse Cyr, a foe of Long's, took the governor's oath before a notary public on the theory that Long's election to the Senate vacated the governor's office. The Kingfish, having prevented Cyr's takeover by calling out the National Guard, maintained that since Cyr had taken the governor's oath he had deprived himself of his rights to the office of lieutenant governor, and that A. O. King, president pro tem of the State Senate and third in line to the governorship, automatically had become lieutenant governor. By a coincidence, King happened to be a member of the Long organization. The whole situation lapsed into low comedy when W. L. Aldrich, a private citizen with a sense of humor, also took the governor's oath. "Since there are two governors," Aldrich said, "I see no reason why we shouldn't have three!" Less amusing—since it demonstrated that Long's hold on the state extended even to the judiciary—was the decision of the Louisiana Supreme Court. It ruled in favor of A. O. King, adopting Long's incredible theory which deprived Cyr of the lieutenant governorship on the ground that he had pressed an unconstitutional claim to the office of governor. Justice St. Paul said:

> This court has no more authority to inquire into the title of Huey P. Long . . . than would a court of the United States be authorized to inquire into the title of Herbert Hoover, to the office of President of the United States.[14]

President Hoover was not asked to comment on the case, but it is doubtful that he would have appreciated either the reasoning or the analogy. . . . Long postponed his move to Washington until 1932 when O. K. Allen, a Long protégé, was elected governor.

Disability

The reported cases on the problem of gubernatorial disability—there are only two—differ from the Garfield and Wilson situations because the determination of inability was made by the courts, not by a cabinet. The case of Governor David H. Goodall of New Hampshire, which deals with the subject at some length, affords the better example.

Governor Goodall became ill early in 1890. By March 31 his condition was such that he wrote to his attorney general:

> Please take such steps as you think necessary to cause the president of the senate to exercise the powers of the office of governor during the vacancy caused by my illness. I am not able to perform the duties of the office, and public service should not suffer from my inability.[15]

Upon receipt of this letter the attorney general petitioned the Supreme Court of New Hampshire for a writ of mandamus to compel the president of the senate to exercise the executive powers and duties. Chief Justice Charles Doe's opinion is the classic one in this field:

> From 1784 to 1792 the governor (then styled President of the State of New Hampshire) was president of the senate. Instead of his present power of vetoing or approving bills passed by the senate and house, he had "a vote equal with any other member" of the senate and also "a casting vote in

case of a tie," and when his office was vacant all his powers were exercised by "the senior senator." When the constitution took effect and the legislature met for the inauguration of the new government, June 2, 1784, Meshech Weare, the governor-elect, was unable to be present. In brief periods of his illness and absence, in June, 1784, and February, 1785, his duties were performed by Woodbury Langdon, senior senator, *acting as governor pro tem*. On both occasions Langdon presided in the senate, by virtue of his provisional tenure of the governor's office; and on the 8th of June, 1784, as governor, he sat with the council, and exercised the governor's power (with the required advice and consent of the council) of signing warrants for the payment of money. . . . The authority of this precedent has not been shaken, and it does not appear that the soundness of the contemporaneous construction has ever been doubted.[16]

The period of New Hampshire history to which Chief Justice Doe referred coincided with the holding of the Federal Convention in 1787 and the ratification and operation of the Constitution in 1789. The experience of Governor Weare in New Hampshire in 1784 and what Doe calls "the contemporaneous construction" of the state's disability clause casts considerable light on the thinking of the statesmen of the period. The men who drafted the New Hampshire Constitution of 1784 sought to avert the dangers of an interregnum just as did the delegates to the Federal Convention. The Chief Justice wrote in this connection:

The mischief designed to be prevented was the suspension of executive government by the governor's death, absence from the state, or disability. . . . The prescribed remedy is the duty of a substitute to act in cases of necessity. The services of a substitute may be necessary when the governor's absence or inability is temporary as well as when it is permanent. . . . In article 49, "vacant by reason of his death, absence from the state, or otherwise," has a broader significance if due weight is given to the evidential force of the primary and leading purpose that the executive work shall go on without interruption. An intermittent vacancy, such as occurred in the time of Governor Weare, may occur again; and the evils of an interregnum, which article 49 was intended to prevent, are not to be introduced by technical reasoning or arbitrary rules. . . .[17]

Since Doe wrote this opinion a scant nine years after the Garfield case, the use of the words "technical reasoning" has special significance. By recognizing the difference between temporary and permanent inability, Doe relegated the Tyler decision to the scrap heap so far as its application to state succession laws was concerned.

It is apparent that the Chief Justice felt that politics should not be the primary factor in determining inability, for his opinion continues:

It is proved by medical testimony that the governor is still in the physical condition stated in his letter to the attorney general, and that his disability may be reasonably expected to last a few weeks and perhaps a few months. It is proved by the testimony of the secretary of state and the state treasurer that there is executive business demanding immediate attention, and that the governor's duties should no longer remain unperformed. The case being one of necessity, article 49 directs the president of the senate to exercise executive powers until the governor resumes them.[18]

Since Governor Goodall himself had declared his inability, the court was not faced with a decision regarding determination of that condition. But Chief Justice Doe also considered the problem of the "reluctant chief executive":

There might be a case in which the attorney general would intervene without such request. While a determination of the question of vacancy on a petition of this kind is not legally requisite to call the president of the senate to the executive chair, it may be a convenient mode of avoiding embarrassment that might sometimes arise from doubt and controversy in regard to his authority, and the validity of his acts. The existence of an executive vacancy is a question of law and fact within the judicial jurisdiction. If the defendant exercised executive power without a previous judgment on that question, the legality of his acts could be contested and determined in subsequent litigation, and the judicial character of the question does not depend upon the time when it is brought into court. With adequate legal process, the consideration and decision of such a question may be prospective as well as retrospective.[19]

In stressing that adequate legal process would insure the

consideration and decision on disability *in advance* of the acting governor's assuming power *as well as afterward,* the Chief Justice probably had in mind two writs which are known in legal language as "quo warranto" and "mandamus." A quo warranto action is brought against an officer of the government to determine by what right (quo warranto) he holds office. Mandamus, as the Latin implies, is in the nature of an order to compel him to perform the functions of his office. Either of these modes could be used to bring about a determination of disability by the courts.

The second recorded case concerning gubernatorial disability occurred in Ohio in 1907. The situation here was significantly different, for the governor had not relinquished office voluntarily. In a superficial opinion, the Ohio court showed its ignorance of constitutional law. Scholars are generally agreed that under most constitutional provisions the alternate or substitute officer should determine disability. Henry E. Davis wrote that

In the absence of any designation to the contrary, "it may be taken to be axiomatic that when the Constitution imposes a duty on an officer, to be done by him, he must be the sole judge when and how to do that duty, subject only to his responsibility to the people and to the risk of impeachment if he act corruptly or improperly." . . .[20]

Similarly, former Attorney General Herbert Brownell, in a summary cited by Attorney General Robert F. Kennedy, stated that

By a well-known principle of law, whenever any official by law or person by private contract is designated to perform certain duties on the happening of certain contingencies, unless otherwise specified, that person who bears the responsibility for performing the duties must also determine when the contingency for the exercise of his powers arises. . . .[21]

Nevertheless, the Ohio court held that the extreme illness of the governor did not cause his powers and duties to devolve upon the lieutenant governor because the governor

had not voluntarily relinquished the office. A self-contained Lieutenant Governor could not be expected to assume the function of the Governor upon his own initiative.[22]

Actual practice has given additional weight to *Attorney General v. Taggart*, the New Hampshire decision. Governor John S. Little of Arkansas suffered a nervous breakdown in 1907. Although Little did not resign and was considered governor for the balance of the term, the president and president pro tem of the senate exercised the powers and duties of the office. Governor Chamberlain of Oregon died in 1910 and was succeeded by Frank M. Benson, the secretary of state. When Benson became incapacitated, Jay Bowerman, president of the senate, acted as governor for the remainder of the term.[23] As late as 1935, the New Hampshire court indicated its support of the Taggart case: a unanimous decision by the court made the distinction between temporary and permanent inability and permitted the president pro tem of the senate to act as governor when that officer was absent from the state.[24]

Perhaps the most extended case of gubernatorial disability occurred in Illinois in the late 1930's. Following a heart attack in November, 1938, Governor Henry Horner spent several months in Florida to regain his health. Despite his illness he would not surrender his office. He returned to Illinois in April, 1939. On April 8, just before the state primary, Lieutenant Governor Stelle proclaimed himself acting governor and called for a special session of the legislature to meet on the same day that Governor Horner had convened the lawmakers. However, the official seal was affixed on Governor Horner's call but not on Lieutenant Governor Stelle's proclamation, and when the legislature met, Stelle took his seat as presiding officer of the senate. Subsequently a private citizen brought a mandamus action to compel Stelle to serve as acting governor. The court held that Governor Horner was a necessary party to the suit; he did not reside in the county in which the action was brought, and therefore the court had no jurisdiction. On October 5, 1939, Horner's secretary signed a "disability certificate" and filed it with the secretary of state. The next day Horner died, and Stelle at last was able to step in. Illinois had been without a governor for just a few weeks short of a year.[25]

Two dramatic cases of gubernatorial disability which occurred in 1959 were alike only in that in each instance the incumbent clung grimly to his office. The case of Governor Earl K. Long made headlines the length and breadth of the land for nearly a month. According to an impartial summary of events:

After a week in which [Governor Long] had burst into profanity on two occasions in the state legislature, he was flown from Baton Rouge to Galveston, Texas, May 30 for mental observation in John Sealy Hospital. After medical testimony that Long was mentally ill and likely to injure himself or others, Probate Judge Hugh Gibson of Galveston, at the request of the Governor's wife, Blanche, ordered him held in protective custody at the hospital June 2 pending a court hearing. Long charged in a court petition in Galveston June 12 that he had been drugged in Louisiana, bound and taken to Galveston by force. He was released from John Sealy Hospital June 17 and flown to New Orleans on his promise to enter Ochsner Foundation Hospital there, which he did. Long stormed out of the hospital June 18 and headed for Baton Rouge in a car, but was intercepted . . . by State Police armed with a court order requested by his wife; he was committed to Southeast Louisiana State Hospital at Mandeville. In a move that prevented his wife from opposing his discharge from the hospital Long filed suit June 19 for a legal separation. Prior to a court hearing at Covington, La., June 26 Long discharged the director of state hospitals and the superintendent of the Mandeville institution and named two new officials, who declared him sane and a free man. The court then dismissed the proceedings.[26]

During the period of Long's confinement, Lieutenant Governor Lether Frazer hesitantly took over the gubernatorial duties—"until I learn something else." Attorney General Jack Gremillion declared Frazer was acting governor until Long could resume his job. After being "released" from Mandeville, Long exercised the duties of governor, but his physical and mental condition deteriorated. In September he withdrew from the primary race for governor, ran for lieutenant governor, and was defeated. The following year he ran for Congress, won the nomination, and died nine days later. While the affairs of the state of Louisiana, as well as its prestige, suffered as a result of this unfortunate sequence of events, the episode did at least dramatize luridly the woeful state of our succession laws.

The second case occurred in Nebraska. On April 17, 1959, Governor Ralph G. Brooks suffered a stroke while en route in a plane from Kansas City to Lincoln. The attack was first characterized as "influenza," then as "diabetes and complete exhaustion," then as a "slight stroke," and finally on May 1 as "cerebral thrombosis."[27] Brooks's prolonged absences because of ill health were toted up in an editorial on April 28, 1960: during his seventeen months in office, the Governor had "been hospitalized for 47 days and off the job for health reasons for a total of about three months."[28] On August 24, 1960, Brooks was again hospitalized for treatment of a virus infection; it affected his heart and his condition was termed critical on August 30.[29] At this time he was a candidate for the United States Senate, but Brooks refused to withdraw from the campaign. The deadline for withdrawal was 5:00 P.M., September 9. At 3:20 P.M. on that day, in spite of the fact that his lungs were filling with fluid, the Governor announced that he was "sticking in the Senate race." He died twenty minutes after making the announcement.[30]

During Brooks's last illness there was no agreement on the procedure for determining disability. The attorney general's office issued no official opinion, although that officer commented to the press that "it was up to the Governor." Lieutenant Governor Dwight Burney said that any citizen could call a hearing before the attorney general; the attorney general denied this; the Governor's administrative assistant said that the whole problem was a medical question. Lieutenant Governor Burney was advised informally that he could determine the Governor's disability himself, but he was afraid of the public reaction and the political consequences that would follow such a step, since he was a Republican and Brooks a Democrat.[31]

In 1961 the Nebraska Legislature passed a bill which created a board of three men to determine disability. Two members are to be doctors and the third is the state's chief justice.[32] Oregon recently passed a similar law creating a disability board composed of the chief justice, the superintendent of the state hospital at Salem, and the dean of the University of Oregon Medical College.[33]

The constitutions of only three states—Alabama, Mississippi, and New Jersey—mention the method of determining disability. In Alabama the supreme court makes the determination, but can act only in cases of "unsoundness of mind." In Mississippi the secretary of state submits the question to the supreme court, and in New Jersey the supreme court decides, but the legislature instigates the action.[34] Although the constitutions of Texas and Alaska provide for the procedure to be prescribed by the legislature, to date these bodies have taken no action.

Commenting on the present practice of the states in his 1961 opinion, Attorney General Kennedy noted that

today with very few exceptions, State Constitutions expressly or impliedly provide that where the governor is unable to exercise the powers and duties of his office, the officer next in line of succession shall discharge them, but only temporarily.*

The inferences to be drawn from this review of State practice and experience relating to gubernatorial disability and its bearing upon this problem of presidential inability have been summarized forcefully by Professor Kallenbach: ". . . State experience reinforces the point observable in national experience that situations of various kinds can and do arise involving inability of the Chief Executive to exercise his powers and which require devolution of these powers for an indefinite period of time upon the officer next in line of succession. It shows that constitutional provisions on this point are, in effect, self-executing. It shows that devolution of power in these circumstances can be brought about by simple acquiescence of the incumbent when he is able to recognize his incapacity. He does not, by so doing, remove himself from office, but merely acquiesces in the operation of the constitutional rule that permits and requires the succeeding officer to exercise the powers of chief executiveship. The officer named by the constitution or laws as the one upon whom the authority to act as governor shall

---

*According to Joseph E. Kallenbach, *Presidential Inability*, House Committee Print, 84th Cong. 2nd Sess. (1956), p. 40, forty-six states have such provisions.

devolve has no option but to exercise the powers and duties of that office, even though his doing so does not oust the incumbent from the office of governor permanently. His duty to so act is an ancillary and conditional function of the incumbent in the office next in line in the succession. When and if the cause occasioning the temporary devolution of power has ceased to be operative, there must be a resumption of his constitutional powers and duties by the temporarily displaced Chief Executive. His assertion of his right and capacity to reassume the powers and duties of his office is ordinarily regarded as sufficient to restore them to him."[35]

The fact remains, however, that more than half the states have no procedure for determining when disability exists, and there is considerable confusion over the whole question. Many of the state officials queried in a recent survey believed that the state supreme court could determine disability by mandamus or quo warranto proceeding; others felt that such a procedure was inadequate.[36]

State court decisions on succession make it apparent that the "melting pot" label is appropriate to describe our legal growth as well as our social and genealogical development. The rulings reflect a variety of components, and the words of the judges often provide clues to the disparate personalities of the governors. In the Huey Long episode in Louisiana, political pressure is manifest in the legal language, but such cases are indeed the exception.

An examination of state cases yields four general conclusions:

(1) Few men will voluntarily give up the office of governor unless by so doing they improve their political position. A sick executive will stay in office regardless of the public interest, while the lieutenant governor stands helplessly by, waiting for death to determine disability.

(2) The state judiciary, on the other hand, repudiates by implication such action by the governor. When a case reaches court, the judges uniformly hold that there should be no lapse of executive power—that vigor in the executive is an essential of good government. If sometimes the judges have done violence to the letter of state laws, or even the

state constitution, it has been in order to uphold one of the most ancient principles of Anglo-American law—the public interest demands that there shall be no interregnum in the executive.

(3) To implement this general purpose the courts have interpreted the succession paragraph to affirm and reaffirm precedents established as early as Jamestown. They have adapted the old practice of deputizing the lieutenant governor, the successor now being designated "acting governor." The Tyler precedent has a few adherents among the states' judiciaries, but its existence is seldom recognized.

(4) By disregarding the Tyler precedent, the state courts have been able to act freely in distinguishing between temporary and permanent inability. They have acted as our forefathers looked to us to do, using experience and wisdom to adapt the state constitutions to modern needs.

Chapter VII

A Basis for Action

Since the final solution to the problems of presidential inability inevitably depends on congressional action, it may not be amiss to review the record of congressional considerations of this matter. As summarized by Ruth Silva, it is not very heartening:

The constitutional provision for the exercise of presidential power during periods of inability received practically no attention until the serious and prolonged illness of President Garfield. The [Presidential Succession] Act of 1792 did not deal with inability; and the poorly reported debates do not show that the Congress even discussed the matter at the time the law was passed. In 1856, when the Senate Committee on the Judiciary was commissioned to study the whole succession problem, the Committee did not consider this particular aspect of the subject. At least, presidential inability was not mentioned in the Committee's report. After President Garfield's illness of eighty days, the Forty-seventh, the Forty-eighth, and the Forty-ninth Congresses discussed the meaning of "inability," its extent and duration, and how it should be established. Instead of dealing with the problem which had so recently alarmed the country, however, the Congress named a statutory successor to act as President during periods of vacancy or inability in the offices of both President and Vice President.

After the enactment of this law the subject of presidential inability was again neglected until the illness of President Wilson. During the eighteen months of his disability, proposals for dealing with the situation were introduced in the Congress, but all were killed in committee. When presidential succession was discussed in the Seventy-ninth and the Eightieth Congresses, inability was presented as the real problem. It was then urged that a joint committee be established to examine all aspects of presidential succession. But the Congress created no such committee, ignored all questions connected with inability, and legislated without benefit of an extensive study.

In terms of actual occurrence inability is the most pressing problem involved in presidential succession. Presidential power has never passed to a statutory successor; but two cases of inability have jeopardized the public interest. Yet Congress has enacted three laws establishing a statutory line of succession and has done nothing to provide for cases of disability. . . .[1]

The unavailing efforts in more recent years to secure congressional action have been described in preceding chapters, and as this book goes to press it appears unlikely that a bill on presidential inability will be passed during the second session of the Eighty-seventh Congress.

Apathy and indifference undoubtedly have been responsible in great part for a century of legislative inaction, but it would be unfair to say that this is still the case. While it is true that too many members of Congress are unaware of the numerous ramifications of the problem, those who are sincerely concerned and who have made a serious attempt to explore it have felt, as Senator Kefauver points out, honest doubt as to the form which either a constitutional amendment or a statute should take. Silva has stated that "the principal reason for neglect of this subject seems to be the difficulty of finding a solution which would be adequate, constitutional, and desirable."[2] It might be added that history, common sense, and the pressures of our time demand that a sound legislative program provide a plan for determining presidential inability which is "swift, small, and uncomplicated" as well as trustworthy.[3]

The procedural and substantive difficulties inherent in the problem can perhaps be stated most clearly in question form: (1) Is a constitutional amendment necessary or can the gap be filled by statute? and (2) What should be the content of either the amendment or the statute?

These were the questions to which the *Nebraska Law Review* addressed itself in a research project which had its inception in September, 1960, at a time when President Eisenhower's illnesses, the carnival case of Governor Earl Long, and the fatal illness of Governor Ralph Brooks were very much in the foreground. During the course of this nineteen-month study of presidential and gubernatorial disability, which was directed by the present writer, a detailed investigation was undertaken of every disability case to reach the courts—and many which did not. The constitutions of all the states in the Union were scrutinized, and colonial precedents were unearthed and carefully perused for the first time. This study, the most comprehensive yet made, led to several conclusions which may prove useful in finding that much-needed "swift, small, and uncomplicated" plan for determining presidential disability.[4]

1. THE PROPOSED AMENDMENT

Is an Amendment Necessary?

The failure of attempts to enact inability legislation, as Senator Kefauver has indicated, has resulted as much from confusion over procedure as from disagreements on substantive provisions: the Congress has never been certain whether the gap can be closed by a passage of a law, or whether a constitutional amendment is required.

There is a natural reluctance to make changes in our basic governmental blueprint. This was the feeling expressed by former President Hoover in a letter of March 15, 1962: "It seems to me that an amendment to the Constitution should be avoided." And he then asked: "Could not an act of Congress duly signed by the President serve the purpose?"*[5] Herbert Brownell's reasoning is relevant to this query:

Ordinary legislation would only throw one more doubtful element into the picture, for the statute's validity could not be tested until the occurrence of the presidential inability, the very time at which uncertainty must be precluded. Most of the proposals involve a transfer or diminution of the Vice President's constitutional power and no statute can do this. Thus, a statute which contained the additional measures needed—a designation of persons to share with the Vice President the power to make the initial decision, or a provision for a solution of disputes between the President and Vice President—would alter the existing powers of the President and Vice President. Even a statute which sought

---

*After studying the proposal by Cornelius W. Wickersham (see page 117), Mr. Hoover wrote to Mr. Wickersham that he felt the amendment proposed is "the most interesting to date."

to do nothing more than declare the original intent of the framers would have to be construed in the light of previous constitutional interpretations and the precedents based on those interpretations, and would therefore be valueless in resolving doubt and uncertainty.[6]

A majority of scholars favor an amendment to the Constitution.* Their conclusion is reinforced by the review of congressional considerations of inability which opens this chapter: as Silva has pointed out, several federal succession statutes have been enacted, not one of which has faced up to the problem of disability. Moreover, the experience of the states since 1789 indicates a reluctance to adopt a statutory solution in the absence of a clear-cut constitutional authority.**

Those who assert that provision for presidential disability may be accomplished by statute would seem to find support in some state constitutions. In the Nebraska Constitution, for example, the wording of the disability clause is such that disability legislation could be enacted by the legislature under the authority given it by the State Constitution to adopt "all laws necessary to carry into effect the provisions of this Constitution" (Nebraska Constitution, Art. XVII, Sec. VI). The Constitution of the United States has a similar "necessary and proper" clause, but the disability clause itself bars statutory action. According to Article II, Section I, Clause 5,

*"Among those who recently expressed themselves in favor of an amendment to the Constitution upon the ground that it is either necessary or desirable are: Stephen K. Bailey, Hon. Peter Frelinghuysen, Richard C. Huber, Joseph E. Kallenbach, Arthur Krock, Jack W. Peltason, C. Herman Pritchett, Arthur E. Sutherland, Hon. John S. Sparkman (*Presidential Inability*, House Committee Print, 84th Cong., 2nd Sess., pp. 59–63). Edgar Waugh, Charles S. Rhyne" (*Hearing, Special Subcommittee of the House Committee on Problem of Presidential Inability*, 85th Cong., 1st Sess., pp. 127, 191).

**The danger of premature enactment of a statute without exhaustive study of the Constitution involved was pointed out by the author in "One Strike and You're Out," *New Hampshire Bar Journal*, July, 1962. The Nebraska Legislature adopted a gubernatorial disability statute without adequate consideration; subsequent study shows it is subject to attack on at least two sound constitutional grounds.

. . . Congress may by Law provide for the Case of Removal, Death, Resignation or Inability, *both of the President and the Vice President,* declaring what Officer shall then act as President, and such Officer shall act accordingly, until the Disability be removed, or a President shall be elected. (Emphasis added).

Thus because of the peculiar wording of this section, Congress is excluded from the right to act in the case of presidential disability only.

Nonetheless, the minority group supporting a statutory solution continue to base their contention that no constitutional amendment is required on the "necessary and proper" clause.* Cornelius W. Wickersham, past chairman of the Committee on the Federal Constitution of the New York State Bar Association, has commented on their stand in his 1962 article, "Presidential Inability: Procrastination, Apathy and the Constitution":

> Although some who have studied the problem feel that Congress has power to deal with the problem under the "necessary and proper" provisions of the Constitution, others are clearly of the opinion that only a constitutional amendment would be satisfactory. The latter rely on the fact that the "necessary and proper" clause applies only to those matters to which basic policies are laid down in the Constitution and does not authorize Congress to fill gaps in the policies so laid down. The latter view seems to be supported by case law** and furthermore, where a constitutional problem of such vital importance, involving not only legal questions but widespread and national implications, is concerned it would seem to be most unwise and probably of small effect to leave the matter to legislation of doubtful constitutionality.[7]

---

*Among those who currently assert that proposed plans of presidential inability may be carried out by statute are Everett S. Brown, Edward S. Corwin, William F. Crosskey, Charles Fairman, David Fellman, James Hart, Arthur N. Holcombe, Mark DeW. Howe. *Opinions of the Attorneys General,* XLII, No. 5 (August 2, 1961), 31 n.

**See, e.g., *Kansas v. Colorado,* 206 U. S. 46 (1907); *United States v. Harris,* 106 U. S. 629 (1883). These cases state the general proposition that Congress can legislate only on subjects where the power to legislate has been granted by the Constitution.

If a solution to the inability problem should be sought through legislation, it is certain that a lawsuit would be brought to test the validity of any statute passed. And the chances are, as Wickersham and Brownell have pointed out, that the action would be brought at a time when the President was disabled—a time when litigation, whether speedy or prolonged, would be least desirable.

An impressive array of lawyers and political scientists is on the record as favoring a constitutional amendment to settle the inability question. But what are the feelings of the men on Capitol Hill? How does Congress look upon such a solution? What inferences might be drawn from Eisenhower's attempts to secure congressional action?

For a time in 1958 members of the Eisenhower official family were highly skeptical that any inability amendment could be passed. Undoubtedly their thinking was influenced by the shellacking which the administration had just taken when President Eisenhower's proposed amendment was before the Congress. In retrospect, however, it appears that there was nothing wrong with the procedural route; the trouble was that in prescribing the *method* for determining inability, the proposed amendment tried to accomplish too much.

Congress, it is axiomatic, will not pass an amendment which is too complicated or too controversial, and to emphasize method is to emphasize a major area of disagreement.* Moreover, method can be handled by statute at a later date. Since Congress had not yet been sold on the procedure to be followed, the inclusion of the provision on

---

*In answers to questions posed by the House Committee on the Judiciary in March, 1957, five of those polled thought Congress should determine inability, six that the Vice President should be the sole judge, and three that the Cabinet should decide (but then so qualified their answers as to nullify them). A number of others thought that the determination should be made by commissions and boards. See House Committee Print, 85th Cong., 2nd Sess., March 26, 1957, pp. 11–12. The men polled were political scientists whose knowledge of the problem supposedly transcends that of the legislators who would be required to make the final choice and pass a law on the method to be used.

method not only made the measure unnecessarily controversial, but also put the cart before the horse.

Cornelius Wickersham's remarks on this "package deal" kind of proposal bring out a further important point:

. . . some proposals for an amendment . . . endeavor to prescribe the methods to be used for determination of the facts relating to inability and to set up machinery for determination of that question both as to the commencement as well as to its termination. But, the difficulty with this course is that the freezing of any one method into the Constitution would make any necessary future correction extremely difficult because it might require an additional constitutional amendment. It is better constitutional practice to *prescribe the principles to govern action* and to leave to the legislature the selection of methods by which those principles can be best implemented under the "necessary and proper" clause. This gives elasticity without imperiling the basic design. The danger of freezing a particular method is avoided by giving to Congress the power to select the method. Correction or improvement can thus be made at any time by the enactment of new legislation within the framework of the amendment.[8]

Wickersham has captured the spirit of the founding fathers, who recognized that they were neither infallible nor all-knowing and who strove to make the Constitution adaptable to future times. Former President Truman has expressed something of this same idea: "I have always felt that there is great danger in writing too much into the Constitution. We must have a certain flexibility to meet changing conditions."[9] A rigid amendment, incorporating a fixed method, would make future changes unduly complicated and would be out of harmony with the concept of flexibility which pervades the entire Constitution.

What Should an Amendment Include?

Assuming that a constitutional amendment is the only way to settle the inability question beyond any doubt, what should be the scope of such a measure?

The foregoing discussion has provided some positive and negative indications as to what might prudently be included. The experience of the Eisenhower administration and the remarks of Wickersham and Truman demonstrate the desirability of removing from consideration the primary question about the power of Congress to enact *any* method, of emphasizing areas of agreement, and of adhering to principles inherent in our system of government. In the search for a constitutional solution, the differences of opinion are more procedural than substantive; the areas of agreement are numerous and basic. The following listing of them will serve as a guide in staking out the terrain the amendment might cover as well as affording a convenient framework for discussion.

1. *In case of permanent inability—the death of the President, his resignation, his conviction by impeachment, or his removal for other cause—the Vice President succeeds to the Presidency.*

Seven Presidents have established the custom that when a President dies, the Vice President becomes President, not Acting President. Few people seriously argue that when a President dies the Vice President should be considered the "servant or agent of the deceased President." Although it was the essence of colonial practice that the alternate was a deputy, no one suggested that he should become an agent or deputy for a dead man. And although John Tyler's assumption of office in 1841 "might readily have been questioned had historical materials on the framers' intent been on hand, the fact remains that it has been relied on for the proposition that the Vice President becomes President when the elected President dies—a proposition scarcely to be questioned today."[10]

2. *In case of temporary presidential inability, the Vice President succeeds only to the powers and duties of the office as the Acting President, and not to the office itself.*

See pages 16–20. According to Attorney General Kennedy, "almost every student of the Constitution who was recently canvassed to express an opinion" was in agreement on this point.*[11] Wickersham, referring to the differences of

*Included in this group of distinguished scholars of the Constitution were: Stephen K. Bailey, Princeton University; Everett S. Brown, University of Michigan; Edward S. Corwin, Princeton, N. J.; William W.

opinion and confusion in the discussions during the series of congressional hearings after President Eisenhower's illness, remarks that "it seems fair to say that the majority felt that in any event the Vice President should not succeed to the office of President but should only be an Acting President until the disability ended or until a new President was elected . . ."[12]

3. *Upon termination of the President's inability prior to the election, he shall resume office.*

See pages 79, 86, 103–104. In the opinion written for President Kennedy, Attorney General Kennedy comments on the minority position:

Unquestionably, those scholars who claim the Vice President becomes President upon the latter's inability would assert that the Vice President may not be divested of his authority by recovery of, or action thereafter by, the President. In my opinion, this view does violence to the letter and spirit of the Constitution, and would defeat the will of the people.

Former Attorneys General Brownell and Rogers were in agreement that the President could reclaim the discharge of the powers and duties of his office merely by announcing that his inability had terminated, and that he is ready now to execute his office. [See Brownell, "Presidential Disability," p. 204.] In my opinion this interpretation of the Constitution is clearly correct. The force of popular opinion, the people's sense of constitutional propriety, and the co-operation of Congress could be counted on to support the President's decision if he acted properly.[13]

It should be noted, however, that former President Tru-

Crosskey, University of Chicago Law School; Charles Fairman, Law School of Harvard University; David Fellman, University of Wisconsin; Thomas K. Finletter, Esq., New York, N. Y.; James Hart, University of Virginia; Arthur N. Holcombe, Harvard University; Mark DeW. Howe, Law School of Harvard University; Richard G. Huber, Tulane University; Joseph E. Kallenbach, University of Michigan; Jack W. Peltason, University of Illinois; J. Roland Pennock, Swarthmore College; C. Herman Pritchett, University of Chicago; John H. Romani, the Brookings Institute; and Arthur E. Sutherland, Law School of Harvard University. *Presidential Inability*, House Committee Print, 85th Cong., 1st Sess. (1957), pp. 49–52." Note appearing in *Opinions of the Attorneys General*, XLII, No. 5 (August 2, 1961), 19–20.

man, in his disability proposal, specified that in the event a President is unable to perform his duties and the Congress by a two-thirds vote designates the Vice President as President, the stricken President would not be able to repossess the office during the remainder of the term, even though he experiences a complete recovery.[14] (See Appendix V for the full text of the Truman proposal.)

4. *The difference between permanent and temporary inability should be clearly stated, recognizing the Tyler precedent in the case of permanent inability and eliminating it as a consideration in the case of temporary inability, which would be governed by (2) above.*

Making a clear-cut distinction between permanent and temporary disability is mandatory before consideration can be given to other aspects of the problem. This step, so long urged, would remedy after nearly 175 years the mistake made by the Committee on Style and restore the original intent of the framers of the Constitution. The experience of the states, as evidenced by the opinions of their courts, has long since indicated the desirability of distinguishing between the various situations. The states have been able to accomplish this through judicial action, but presidential disability, existing solely within the confines of the executive branch, is removed from determination by the courts or Congress.

In view of the questions raised by the Garfield and Wilson Cabinets, it might be well to define the legal status of a disabled President during the period a Vice President acts as President. Such a rationale may not be necessary, but the question of "how . . . the duties can be separated from the office"[15] has arisen many times in state and national history, and it would be reassuring to have this dilemma concisely resolved. The explanation given by Justice Alexander Anderson of California has been overlooked for many years because the case dealt with the temporary disability (absence) of a justice, not a governor. However the same principle applies. Justice Anderson said:

. . . the vested rights of the term attaches to the person of the elected incumbent, but . . . the functions of the office, in certain contingencies, separate from him temporarily, and adhere to a distinct class of powers within the department, for the use, benefit and protection of that great public for which the government was created.[16]

5. Commencement and termination of a disability shall be determined by such method as Congress shall by law provide, so long as that method is compatible with the system of checks and balances provided for in the Constitution for the maintenance of the separate and coequal branches of the government.

Students of the presidential disability problem will find in the many and various proposals for its solution repeated affirmations of the necessity for maintaining a balance between the three branches of the government, assuring continuation of the traditional checks which one has against the other, and preventing the dominance of one over the other. For examples, one needs only to look to the writings of our living former Presidents. Truman's suggested method for determining presidential disability involves "representatives of the three branches of government"; Hoover believes that "the method of determining 'inability' or 'recovery' requires consideration of the spirit of the separation of powers in the Government . . ."; and Eisenhower's position in this regard, which was made abundantly clear to the author in a personal interview, has been well expressed by members of his administration. His concern lest "a major shift in the checks and balances among the three divisions of the government . . . result" is stressed by former Attorney General Brownell.[17]

Senator Kefauver, in the introduction to this book, makes it clear that the legislative branch is no less interested in preserving the separation of powers; and Chief Justice Warren, speaking for the Supreme Court, gave this doctrine as the primary reason why members of the Court should not serve on any disability commission (see page 71).

The disability clause should be and must be harmonized with the Twentieth Amendment. The so-called Lame Duck amendment recognizes the distinction between temporary and permanent disability by providing that if, at the time fixed for beginning the term of the President, the President-elect has died, then the Vice President-elect "shall become President." The amendment further provides that if a President has not been chosen by the time fixed for the beginning of his term, or if a President-elect fails to qualify, then the Vice President-elect shall "*act* as President until the President qualifies" (see page 19). As the Constitution now stands, the disability clause, the interpretation put upon it by seven Presidents, and the Twentieth Amendment are at odds with each other.

These five areas of agreement are embodied in the following proposal for an amendment made by the Committee on the Federal Constitution of the New York State Bar Association:

In case of the Removal of the President from Office, or of his Death or Resignation, the said Office shall devolve on the Vice President. In Case of the Inability of the President to Discharge the Powers and Duties of the said Office, the said Powers and Duties shall devolve on the Vice President, until the Inability be Removed. The Congress may by law provide for the Case of Removal, Death, Resignation or Inability, both of the President and Vice President, declaring what Officer shall then be President, or in case of Inability, act as President, and such Officer shall be or act as President accordingly, until a President shall be elected, or, in the case of Inability, until the Inability shall earlier be removed. The commencement and termination of any Inability shall be determined by such method as Congress shall by law provide.*[18]

This proposal could be readily expanded to include the proposed rationale for the distinction between temporary and permanent disability. So that there would be no possibility for further confusion about the scope of the powers given to Congress, it would seem wise to remove the word "both"; and it would, of course, be essential to add a qualifying clause to the last sentence: "so long as that method is compatible with the system of checks and balances and the maintenance of the three separate and coequal branches of government."

*See also Appendix III, Proposal of *Nebraska Law Review.*

In such a form, the amendment would be logical and on sound ground historically and legally. It would, in the author's opinion find support from scholars, past and present Attorneys General, and the former Presidents. With such support, the prospect of passage of the amendment would be far more favorable than before. Once it had been adopted by Congress, ratification by two-thirds of the states could be anticipated within ten to twelve months.

Contrary to popular opinion, "amending the Constitution" need not be a process prolonged over a period of years. The Seventeenth Amendment, providing for the election of senators by popular vote, took thirteen and a half months; the Nineteenth (woman suffrage) fifteen months; and the Twenty-first (repealing the Eighteenth Amendment) less than ten months. The public's increasing awareness of the urgency of inability legislation no doubt would expedite the process in the present case.

2. THE DETERMINATION OF INABILITY

After the amendment has been ratified, it would be up to the Congress to choose a sound method for determining inability. While passage of an amendment of the type discussed above would not automatically insure a quick agreement on the *modus operandi,* there would be a climate of cooperation and accomplishment far more conducive to productive action than the present rather competitive atmosphere.

Should Determination of Inability Remain within the Executive Branch?

Most of the procedures proposed to date have suggested that the determination of inability be made by the legislative branch, the Supreme Court, or a combination of the two with officials from the executive branch.* In this con-

---

*The American Bar Association's Standing Committee on Jurisprudence and Law Reform has proposed a commission with representatives from all three branches. The proposal is questionable on several counts, including possible violation of the separation of powers doctrine.

nection the suggested constitutional provision requiring compatibility with the doctrine of separation of powers becomes a paramount consideration. Which of these procedures is compatible with the maintenance of three separate, coordinate, and coequal departments of government? Let us consider the methods proposed in the light of this basic requirement.

It has frequently been suggested that the Supreme Court would offer an impartial forum of respected men who could determine presidential inability. Study of proposals incorporating this view shows that they not only would violate the doctrine of separation of powers, but would be eminently impractical. It will be remembered that two Chief Justices, Roger B. Taney and Earl Warren, rejected suggestions that they take part in the succession procedure at any stage (see pages 11 and 71). Taney, in refusing to confer on the question of whether or not Tyler was to take the oath prescribed for the President, said in part that he wanted to be careful lest it appear he was intruding in the business of a coordinate branch of the government. Warren, in his letter to Representative Keating, requested that the members of the Supreme Court be excluded from participating in the determination of inability. The sound legal basis for this request has been illustrated by Wickersham:

The policy of the federal courts to avoid political questions was well expressed by Mr. Justice Frankfurter in *Colegrove v. Green* [328 U. S. 549, 553–54] as follows:

> From the determination of such issues this Court has traditionally held aloof. It is hostile to a democratic system to involve the judiciary in the politics of the people. And it is not less pernicious if such judicial intervention in an essentially political contest be dressed up in the abstract phrases of the law.

Thus, it is safe to assume that neither *quo warranto* nor *mandamus* is available in a federal court. Aside from the basic question of the correct interpretation of the Constitution, solution by court action presumably cannot be relied upon.

Even if the courts were willing to take jurisdiction it might require months of litigation before a final decision was reached. During that time no officer of the Government would be sure of his right to carry out the order given to him by either of the claimants. The result could easily be a complete paralysis of our Government and of its armed forces in case of war, rebellion or invasion.[19]

Wickersham further points out that the disability question came before the Supreme Court of New Hampshire in the Taggart case (see pages 96 ff.) because the attorney general instigated the action at the request of the governor himself. Wickersham's clear implication is that if the governor had been unconscious, or had not initiated the action by his letter to the attorney general, or had in fact opposed such action, the court would have hesitated to assume jurisdiction. That Wickersham's implication is justified by practical experience is shown by the Ohio case (see page 99) in which the State Supreme Court refused jurisdiction because the action was not initiated by the governor. The experience of the United States with its Presidents and governors is replete with examples which substantiate Wickersham's argument that a chief executive may not step aside voluntarily, and that failing such action by the incumbent the courts may refuse to take jurisdiction.

Noel Dowling, Professor Emeritus of Constitutional Law at Columbia University has put forward a second and even more cogent reason for excluding the Supreme Court from any statutory scheme of determining disability: the original jurisdiction of the Supreme Court does not include such matters. Under the present Constitution, the United States Supreme Court would not issue a mandamus or quo warranto proceedings as was done in the Taggart case; a constitutional amendment would be required to give them that power.[20] Would such action be practical?

The wisdom of removing the justices from consideration for any inability commission is supported historically by the Hayes-Tilden election dispute of 1876. In the presidential election of that year, the balloting in several states and the counting and tabulating of the vote, was so clearly characterized by fraud on both sides that it was impossible to determine which of the nominees was entitled to the electoral votes of those states. Congress consequently created a special commission to pass judgment on the disputed votes. The commission was composed of five senators (three Republicans and two Democrats), five members from the House of Representatives (three Democrats and two Republicans), and five justices of the Supreme Court. It was intended that there be two Republicans and two Democrats from the last-named body, and the deciding vote was to go to Justice David Davis of Illinois, an Independent. But Davis was unexpectedly elected to the Senate, and resigned from the Court to accept the office. Since the remaining justices were all Republicans, the commission decided the election disputes in Hayes's favor by a straight eight-to-seven party-line vote. Millions of Americans were infuriated at this demonstration of partisan politics by supposedly non-partisan Supreme Court justices, and for more than twenty years the Court was criticized for taking part in the resolution of the question. No doubt the Warren Court had this affair in mind when it pointed out the impropriety of its members serving on a disability commission—and of course the legal arguments presented by Warren have a basis which no one has been able to refute.

Former President Truman has advocated deciding inability by a vote of the Congress. In 1957 he proposed that

when a President is stricken with an illness . . . there should come into being a Committee of Seven composed of representatives of the three branches of the Government. . . . This Committee would select a board of leading medical authorities drawn from top medical schools of the Nation. This medical board, thus chosen, would then make the necessary examinations, presenting their findings to the Committee of Seven. Should the findings of the medical board indicate that the President is unable to perform his duties, and that he is, in fact, truly incapacitated and not merely stricken with a transitory illness, then the Committee of Seven would so inform the Congress. Congress would then have the right to act, and by a two-thirds vote of the full membership declare the Vice President as President.[21]

This proposal would hardly assure swift and decisive action. Nor would the public place confidence in a nonpolitical decision by a body which, by its very nature, is political. After the experience with Congress during the Johnson impeachment trial, few scholars support the proposal.

The Federal Convention itself refused to enlarge the powers of Congress over the executive. When the delegates discussed impeachment procedure, it was suggested that the practice of the states be followed: that, is, when impeachment charges are filed, the President (like the governors) be suspended pending the outcome of the trial. James Madison, the father of the Constitution, objected in these words:

> The President is made too dependent already on the Legislature, by the power of one branch to try him in consequence of an impeachment by the other. This intermediate suspension will put him in the power of one branch only. They can, at any moment, in order to make way for the functions of another who will be more favorable to their views, vote a temporary removal of the existing magistrate.[22]

Madison won his point and the Convention refused to extend the power of Congress over the President. The vote was three states to eight. The analogy to disability is clear: temporary removal of an executive could be accomplished as easily by letting Congress decide his disability. Congress would not need to impeach a President; they could declare him permanently disabled! The same principle is involved and the same reasoning should apply in rejecting any such proposal.

History, experience, and common sense dictate that, if we are to preserve the doctrine of separation of powers and maintain three separate and coequal departments of government, the determination of presidential inability must remain within the executive branch. In Herbert Brownell's words:

> If the power of initial determination is diverted from the executive branch, or even is shared in some fashion with those outside the executive, a way is opened for harassment of a President for political motives. A major shift in the checks and balances among the three divisions of the federal government could well result.[23]

Should the Vice President Determine Inability?

The evolution which has taken place in the office of Vice President is suggested by a comparison of the role of Chester A. Arthur, who was excluded from the deliberations of the Cabinet during Garfield's illness, and the part played by Richard Nixon during Eisenhower's sicknesses. One might even say there was a trend for the Vice President to revert to the status of the "Deputie Governour" of the colonial period, and the Eisenhower and Kennedy agreements could be characterized as an attempt by the President to "deputize" the Vice President, even as the colonial governors deputized their alternates. Unless the legal procedure for choosing our Vice Presidents is modified, or unless there is a change which would eliminate his ties to Congress and place him solely in the executive branch (Hoover's suggestion that he become an Assistant President), it is reasonable to expect that modern Presidents will continue to delegate as many duties as legally possible to the Vice President. He will no doubt continue to sit in on Cabinet meetings, and the trend toward deputization probably will increase rather than diminish. Thus, the Vice President will be much better trained to succeed to the Presidency than were his predecessors.

But if the office of Vice President has changed, the system of choosing the Vice President has not. Tyler, as we have seen, became Vice President because of a political deal with Clay; Arthur's nomination was an attempt to placate the Stalwart faction; Marshall admittedly was Wilson's second choice. In recent times the President's potential successor too often has been chosen on the basis of geography, and the presidential ticket is still too often a marriage of convenience. It is by no means inconceivable that a personal or political antagonism could develop between some future President and his running mate.

In planning for disability, how can the growth of the Vice Presidency be recognized on the one hand, and its static potential for disagreements on the other? Perhaps the answer is indicated by the common denominator in the conduct of Vice Presidents during presidential disability. In the three major instances of temporary inability, Vice Presidents Arthur, Marshall, and Nixon made no attempt to determine disability, although at least Nixon had reason to believe the legal right was his.

Since history has shown that the Vice President will not initiate action for determining inability, why not remove him completely from this determination? He would then come into office, temporarily or permanently, not only well versed in the business of the executive department but free from the personal embarrassment and public criticism which would attend his passing upon his own advancement.

What Should Be the Cabinet's Role?

In his letter to Senator Kefauver (the full text appears in Appendix V), former President Hoover pointed out that "the President and Vice President are elected as the chosen leaders of a political party with declared mandates, principles, solutions of issues, and promises to the people." But an opposition political party may—and frequently does—control one or both of the Houses of Congress, in which case those in control "are, in practice, mostly opposed to the mandates or promises upon which the President and Vice President are elected by the people. All of which leads me to the generalization that a President's inability to serve . . . should be determined by the leading officials in the executive branch, as they are of the party having the responsibilities determined by the election."[24]

Certainly the political consequences of presidential illnesses cannot be overlooked, but any method for determining disability must take into account that the issue is primarily *medical*, not political. Election to the Presidency of the United States does not change a man's anatomy or physiology; he is still mortal, with lungs, heart, digestive and nervous systems like the rest of us. The former Presidents themselves are the first to bear testimony to this fact. Eisenhower has shown by his rigid adherence to the regimen prescribed by his doctors that he recognizes the critical role played by medical men in keeping a President fit. Truman recommended that his "Committee of Seven" select "a board of leading medical authorities drawn from the top medical schools of the nation";[25] and Hoover in his letter suggested that a commission made up of chief officials of departments or agencies within the executive branch "should seek the advice of a panel of experienced physicians or surgeons" in determining inability.[26]

During the illnesses of Garfield and Eisenhower it was the Cabinet which ran the government of the United States, and it was the Cabinet, along with Dr. Grayson and Mrs. Wilson, which presided over the operations of the executive during Wilson's long incapacity. During Wilson's illness two bills were introduced to give the Cabinet the power to determine inability.* According to Silva,

Hearings on these bills disclosed the belief that the Cabinet is the safest body in which to vest the power. Determination by the Cabinet would cause the least friction because the decision would be made by the President's own appointees. Cabinet members presumably are his friends and are not eager to displace him. Moreover, the Cabinet is in the best position to know whether a President is really disabled or not.[27]

But the Wilson case reminds us that there is always the possibility that the palace guard can play a "house game" and fail to brief the Cabinet fully on the President's condition. Nor can we forget that Wilson's Secretary of State was compelled to resign because he had convened the Cabinet.

The historical difficulties in leaving the determination of inability to the Cabinet could be obviated if an impartial medical board were to be established (see below). The board

---

*H.R. 12629, introduced by Martin B. Madden of Illinois, and H.R. 12647, introduced by Clifton N. McArthur of Oregon, 66th Congress. "The Madden bill provided that, whenever the President became unable to perform his duties for six consecutive weeks, the question of his inability was to be made the subject of official inquiry by the Cabinet. The bill empowered the Secretary of State to convene the Cabinet for this purpose, and provided that the determination was to be made by a majority vote. The removal of a disability was to be established in the same manner. The McArthur bill contained similar provisions. Madden thought his bill superior to McArthur's because it made the Secretary of State legally responsible for calling the Cabinet together in case of a President's inability. He objected to Wilson's ruling that a President's inability prevented the Cabinet from functioning" (Silva, *Presidential Succession*, p. 108 n.).

would inform the Cabinet *and the public* of the President's condition, and the Cabinet, exclusive of the Vice President, would make the final determination of disability or recovery, using the report of the board as a guide to both instances.

Is a Medical Board Necessary? How Would It Operate?

Evidence of the increasingly large part doctors play in relation to the Presidency can be found in the extralegal physical examinations of present-day Chief Executives. That such examinations take place is a tacit, if not express, admission that perhaps preventive medicine should apply to a President as well as corporation executive. The trend for presidential candidates to take physical examinations is also indicative of the growing awareness on the part of both politicians and voters that the people of the United States have an interest in the President's general health as well as his condition if he should be ill.

But the fact remains that presidential physical examinations are still discretionary, and what the public is told of the results of such examinations is still up to the President and his official family. Moreover presidential physicians are usually personal friends of the President, biased in his favor to a greater or lesser extent. We have seen that Dr. Grayson told a series of half-truths to Wilson's Cabinet; that the initial diagnosis of a coronary thrombosis was overridden by Harding's personal physician, General Sawyer; that Cleveland's cancer operation was concealed from all but one of his Cabinet members, to say nothing of the public (Dr. John F. Erdman later observed that at the time of the Cleveland operation and convalescence "he did more lying than in all the rest of his life put together"[28]); that at least two twentieth-century Presidents—Wilson and Franklin Roosevelt—ignored the advice of their physicians with disastrous consequences; and that Roosevelt, according to his own son, did not inform Dr. Ross T. McIntire of two seizures.

Surely these lessons of history and human nature point to the necessity of enacting legislation requiring periodic physical examinations of the President by a board of physicians. But how can such a procedure be kept within the executive branch and at the same time removed from presidential domination?

An answer is suggested in the example of the organization of the Secret Service, which protects the President from outside threats to his life and well-being. The White House Detail is responsible to the Secretary of the Treasury, who in this regard is in turn responsible to the Congress, not to the President. The Secret Service may veto presidential activities which might endanger the Chief Executive's life, and though there are times when they resent the interference and inconvenient precautionary measures "Presidents usually accept the laws of the land and follow Secret Service advice with little or no question."[29] The organization of the Secret Service could, by analogy, provide the rationale for setting up an impartial board of physicians charged with the responsibility of protecting the President from ills, including that of overworking himself. The Secretary of Health, Education, and Welfare could select the doctors on a rotating basis from a list provided by the Civil Service Commission. The board of physicians would be responsible to the Secretary, who in turn would be responsible to the Congress, not the President, for the health of the Chief Executive—just as the Secretary of the Treasury is responsible to the Congress for his safety.

Doctors uniformly recommend at least one comprehensive physical a year for the average adult male. It would be reasonable to require quarterly physicals for the President, with the board automatically stepping in when there is a major illness. "Major illness" could be determined by the President's personal physician, his family, or the Cabinet. Or, if the board felt there was sufficient question about the President's health, it could determine by a majority vote to conduct an examination. It is highly unlikely that the board would act capriciously in conducting such an examination; most people would consider it more disinterested than the Cabinet or the President's family. Referring to the proposed commission made up of high officials from the executive branch which would determine inability, Hoover said that he could not "conceive of any circumstance when such a defined body of leaders . . . would act in these circumstances other than in the national interest." The traditions and code of the medical profession are such that surely we should be able to make the same statement about a responsible board of physicians.

It would not be necessary to make public the results of every routine examination. Merriman Smith offers a suggestion, based on observation of four Presidents:

My essential feeling is that aside from recognizedly minor involvements—a cold, a sprain, or something equally trivial—when the illness of a President is sufficiently serious to warrant public announcement, the White House then should make available quite detailed medical information.

When a President has more than a minor ailment, I think the public is entitled to know just how sick he is, entitled to know the basic medical facts in order to arrive at independent judgment. The illness of a President has no right whatever to be a private matter.[30]

Under the impartial medical board proposed, announcement could be made first to the Cabinet, then to the public. The statement to the Cabinet could include a recommendation concerning temporary or permanent disability.

What Are the Objections to a Medical Board?

When the disability problem first came up for discussion in the Eisenhower Cabinet, says Sherman Adams,

Eisenhower suggested that a special committee consisting of the Chief Justice and representatives of the medical profession, among others, should decide. . . . I think that any plan that attempts to prescribe physical examination and reports from a standing group of physicians would be impractical and unwise. The sense of personal responsibility which the President has in keeping fit is as implicit as his feeling of responsibility for conducting the affairs of his office.[31]

By this time—1958—there had been a number of suggestions for disability commissions. Only one of these proposals placed emphasis on the role of the medical profession;* the

*See *Presidential Inability: An Analysis of Replies to a Questionnaire and Testimony at a Hearing on Presidential Inability*, Committee on the Judiciary, House of Representatives, March 26, 1957, p. 21.

others grouped together such diverse categories as Supreme Court justices, inferior court judges, the President's wife, the Cabinet, and party leaders.

Brownell says of these multi-member bodies:

> Arguments for a group determination of presidential inability overlook the fact that throughout American history, not merely in the Garfield and Wilson instances, the problem has never been ascertaining presidential inability; the stalemate in executive activity has proceeded from a Vice President's reluctance to assume his superior's office and a President's (or his personal advisers') reluctance to turn over presidential duties with no assurance of their return.
>
> Not only would such a fact-finding commission have been unnecessary and ineffective in every presidential inability problem so far encountered, but in the future it could have very serious and unfortunate consequences. Any law requiring complicated procedures, investigations, hearings, findings, and votes, would prevent immediate action in case of emergency. Today's need is for unquestioned continuity of executive power and leadership. A law establishing a fact-finding body on this issue might completely thwart that objective, to the nation's deadly peril.
>
> Furthermore, it seems unwise to establish elaborate legal machinery to provide for examinations of the President. The question of the physical and mental capacity one needs to serve as President is, of course, far more than a matter of medical findings by a group of learned physicians. Providing for physical and mental examinations would, at the least, be an affront to the President's personal dignity and degrade the presidential office itself; more dangerously, it would give a hostile group power to harass the President for political purposes.[32]

It is clear that Brownell's objections are addressed generally to the multi-member commissions proposed by various groups; only in the last paragraph quoted does he discuss doctors as the sole determinants of inability. Brownell's belief that "the stalemate in executive activity has proceeded from a Vice President's reluctance to assume his superior's office" and that "the problem has never been ascertaining presidential disability" blandly overlooks that neither Vice

Presidents Marshall nor Arthur were kept informed about the condition of the Chief Executive. Moreover, the idea that the Vice President is the sole person to determine disability was not seriously considered until Davis' article (cited by Brownell, p. 190) was published in 1919, and it was not generally recognized until after Silva's book was published in 1951. Since Brownell was appointed by a President who made no secret of his physical condition it is understandable that the former Attorney General should feel that "the problem has never been ascertaining presidential disability"; but history belies his statement. A review of the lives of our Presidents proves that "the sense of personal responsibility which the President has in keeping fit" has weighed more heavily with some than others. "Duty" has too often been confused with compulsion and it would be interesting to hear a psychiatrist's explanation of the reasons for the almost total disregard, in some cases, for the sound advice of a physician.

Brownell assumes from the various proposals for commissions that they would necessarily require "complicated procedures, investigations, hearings, findings, and votes," making an immediate decision impossible. This conclusion is warranted when some of the proposals advanced are examined carefully. But it would be invalid in the case of an impartial board of physicians, appointed by the Secretary of Health, Education, and Welfare and working within the framework of an organization patterned after that of the Secret Service. Since Brownell's statements in the *Yale Law Journal* had been directed primarily at the hybrid commissions, he was queried regarding the use of doctors in determining disability. His answer was:

These proposals were deemed inadequate for several reasons. One was that if the decision-making power were given exclusively to the medical panel we thought it would be entrusting them with making a kind of decision which does not lie fully within the competence of medical men. The doctors could discover the facts relative to the actual physical or mental condition of the President but the judgment as to whether the President is able to discharge his functions and duties goes beyond medical knowledge and also involves practical governmental experience. Secondly, if the panel were given merely advisory authority it was believed that the particular physical or mental ailment of the President might not come within the competence of the pre-selected physicians; also that irresponsible demands would be made from time to time by prejudiced persons to have physical examinations made of the President, and doubts could be raised either by refusing to have the examination made or by disagreement among the members of the panel or doubt as to the meaning of the panel's report.[33]

Brownell points out that the particular ailment might not come within the competence of the medical board, but this is a rather superficial objection. The board should not be composed of specialists but of general practitioners with authority to call in specialists as needed. Trying to antici-pate every specific ill by putting specialists on the board could result in a body so large it would be grossly imprac-tical. A board of general practitioners should also have the authority to call in the President's personal physician for consultation and for his records.

The former Attorney General has expressed fear of irre-sponsible demands by prejudiced persons, leading to harass-ment of the President for political motives. If the board were composed of doctors from private practice, political pressures might prove irresistible. Politics is not foreign to the medical associations, as the doctors are the first to ad-mit. And an unpopular decision could finish a physician's private practice. Political influence could be held to a mini-mum by providing that the board be chosen from the ranks of the thousands of physicians presently in the Civil Service of the United States—from the staffs of our veterans hos-pitals, for example. The doctors should be far enough re-moved from the top echelon to be free from direct pressure; a double precaution would be to change the personnel of the board after each examination, just as the members of the Secret Service White House Detail are changed from time to time, and always with each new administration. If the organization were patterned after that of the Secret Service, harassment would be unlikely. Brownell has never asserted that the Secret Service men harass the President;

what they do is for his personal safety, and does not consti-
tute "an affront to his personal dignity." In principle, such
an argument could be considered to put personal dignity before the public welfare: it smacks too much of Mrs. Wilson's
statement that she thought of her husband first and the
public good second. When one assumes the Presidency, it is
taken for granted that a large degree of privacy will be lost.

The political implications of a presidential illness, as
already mentioned, could be recognized by leaving the *final*
decision to the Cabinet; the political ties of that body to the
President could be acknowledged by requiring that the
medical report be made public at the time it was given to
the Cabinet. With the eyes of the nation on them, and the
medical facts known to all the parties and the public, a nonpolitical decision would be more likely, if not assured.

Summary: A Method for Determining Disability

The method summarized below is derived from the
Nebraska Law Review's investigation of executive disability.
While this study is the most comprehensive yet to be made,
the following proposal is offered with the full awareness
that no one person or organization can have the ideal answer to such a complex problem, and that compromise will
be essential to the passage of any legislation.

1. The determination of disability should remain within
the executive branch, recognizing that the separation of
powers doctrine, as originally expressed by Madison, upheld
by the Constitutional Convention and ratified by the states,
and perpetuated by subsequent case law proscribes per se
any plan that would place the determination of disability in
the hands of Congress, the Supreme Court, any combination
thereof, or any temporary commission composed of citizens
and government employees.

2. The Vice President should be removed from any participation in the process of determining presidential inability; the trend to inform him and prepare him for succession
should be recognized and implemented by insuring that if
he should be called upon to exercise the duties of President,

he enters upon their execution free from any suspicion of usurpation or precipitate action.

3. While the determination of disability should be kept within the executive department, the necessary machinery should not be under the direct supervision of the President. The precedent existing in the structural composition and organization of the White House Secret Service Detail suggests a very practical solution.

Under a similar plan, physicians from the government service would be appointed to a medical board by the Secretary of Health, Education, and Welfare. The President's personal physician could be an ex officio member of the board, but with no authority to compose or supervise the examination or report, though his records probably would be voluntarily requested by the board and his opinion would rightfully be solicited.

Examinations could be given at stated intervals (at least quarterly) or in case of "major illness," and "major illness" could be quickly determined by a simple majority vote of the doctors, trusting in their professional experience to insure against premature or immature judgment. Following the examination, the doctors could report to the public and the Cabinet concerning the President's state of health.

The Cabinet—and excluding the Vice President or anyone else (the Tumultys of the future)—would have the legal responsibility, with the eyes of an informed American public focused upon them, for making the final decision concerning the President's disability by a simple majority vote.

Current members of the health board could be assigned to the staff of one of the government hospitals in Washington in order to be immediately available in case of a major illness; possibly one of them, as a "Chairman," could be detailed to accompany the President on any trips made; so a report could be made immediately to the board regarding any illness that occurred during the President's absence from Washington.

4. To avoid charges that the legislation proposed is intended to harass or embarrass a President then in office, a clause should be included making the law effective with the President whose term begins following enactment.

The Presidency as it was in the days of Tippecanoe and Tyler is no more. Presidents Truman, Eisenhower, and Kennedy have said again and again that no one can comprehend the scope of the trust placed in the man in the White House unless he himself takes up residence there. Speaking of the need for modernizing the disability clause, Mr. Truman has written:

. . . who could fully foresee the role of the American Presidency in the kind of world in which we now live—a role which also requires the President to be available in person at any hour to make decisions which he alone can make and which cannot be put off?[34]

The President's personal powers are startling, and his exercise of them can affect directly every citizen of the United States. For instance, the President by signing his name can change the value of the dollar in your wallet or purse; if you are a farmer or engaged in work subsidized in some way by the government or if you should be in need of federal disaster relief, the President's inability to sign his name not only could keep money from your pocket but might mean misery for you and your family; if you are a laboring man, the President's action or inaction in a labor dispute can decide whether or not you go to work in the morning; if you are a businessman, the failure of a disabled President to adjust imports at a critical time could ruin your business overnight. But these matters seem trivial when compared with international problems.

The President's powers and responsibilities in the field of foreign affairs are such that the necessity for keeping the President fit, physically and mentally, is synonymous with national survival. The nature of these responsibilities is symbolized by a large leather pouch, with a double lock. Guarded by five United States Army warrant officers,

this pouch contains all the super-secret messages and codes to put the nation's key emergency plans into effect. *These are the plans which only the President can initiate.*

They are not plans for declaring war. They are plans to meet any military challenge to the security of the United States and its allies. The pouch contains the coded key to unleash our retaliatory forces, if we are attacked.[35]

On the President's desk sits a "crash" telephone. A President has only to reach for that telephone, speak a few words in the mouthpiece, and our nuclear deterrent is unleashed. The law as it now stands increases the risk that a sick President either might use that telephone prematurely or be unable to use it at all. It would be a tragic irony if we continued to spend billions for defense but lost the final battle because we chose to gamble with destiny on the wording of one section of the Constitution.

Appendix I

Inability of the President

What Constitutes? and Who Decides?

MONOGRAPH BY HENRY E. DAVIS

NOTE.—The greater portion of the following article was prepared in the summer and autumn of the year 1881, when its subject was of lively interest owing to the attack upon President Garfield. The additions due to the discussion in Congress over the bill which subsequently became law in the form of the act of January 19, 1886, respecting the performance of the duties of the office of President in case of the removal, etc., of both the President and Vice President, will readily be recognized. The reader of the act of January 19, 1886, and of the debates preceding the enactment of the same will observe that notwithstanding the fact that the question treated in the article was very fully discussed, no attempt to settle it was made by Congress and that it is accordingly as open as ever. The article is printed in the form in which it was originally put in final shape, 30 years ago.

The severe and protracted illness of President Garfield brought into prominence a provision of the Federal Constitution which, until that emergency, may be said to have been practically out of sight since the organization of the Government—the provision, namely, respecting the discharge of the duties of the Executive during an inability of the President. (Art. II, sec. 1, cl. 5: "In case of the removal of the President from office, or his death, resignation, or inability to discharge the powers and duties of the said office, the same shall devolve on the Vice President, and the Congress may by law provide for the case of removal, death, resignation, or inability, both of the President and Vice President, declaring what officer shall then act as President, and such officer shall act accordingly until the disability be removed or a President shall be elected.") The cognate provision as to the discharge of those duties on the death of the President had three times been called into requisition—in the cases of Vice Presidents Tyler, Fillmore, and Johnson; that which refers to removal was, for a while, forcibly present to the mind of President Johnson at least; and that respecting resignation was, in all probability, one of the few jests which tempered the almost depressing earnestness of the

Federal convention. But the inability provision slept a long sleep, to be awakened at last by a second "shot heard round the world."

What does that provision mean? was at once the anxious general inquiry; and as the subject presented itself quite as a nova questio, many and various were the replies. Of such as found their way into print scarcely any two agreed; if they seemed to agree in one particular they differed in at least one other, and earnest as was the general discussion represented by these replies no digest of them could approach a harmony.

The question is still as interesting and important as when thus startlingly projected, for while the Congress is even now seeking some solution of the problem of the order of succession in case of inability of both President and Vice President, no effort is making (and it is difficult to perceive how any generally satisfactory effort could be made) by that department of Government to solve the many other problems touching the character, extent, and ascertainment of an inability, and the proper course of action by the officer or officers most nearly concerned.

What the provision means is then of vital interest, and in dealing with the question it is necessary to look closely not only at the provision itself, but also into the object which the framers of the Constitution thought they were attaining by it. And manifestly there are two points of view from which such examination may be made, the first in natural order being that of the proceedings of the convention, the other that of the language of the provision as it left the convention's hands—or, rather, as it now meets the eye; for, as indicated below, there would seem to be reason for this particularity in the form of the statement.

The general disposition has been to confine examination to the language, such resort as has been had to the proceedings being almost exclusively spasmodic and for purposes of illustration on some single point. Conforming for the present to that disposition, it is of interest to consider what may fairly be deemed representative specimens of the varying results of such examination.

The questions which, in this connection, suggest themselves upon the threshold are such as these: What is inability in the sense of the provision; and what its effect as to the Executive and executive duties? Each of these questions includes others: Who shall decide when the inability occurs, whether it is continuing at a given date, when it has ceased? And, in case of inability of the President, does the Vice President become President or merely acting President for the time being? And at the termination of the inability shall the President and the Vice President resume their normal functions?

The difficulties in the way of satisfactory answer to these questions are sufficiently attested by the varying conclusions already adverted to. As a general answer, some say that the inability contemplated by the Constitution is one that shall completely disable the President to discharge his duties during the remainder of his term, in fact, a quasi death; on which the Vice President, on his own decision of the necessity, shall become President; and that any other case of in ability is casus omissus (ex-Judge Dittenhoefer in New York Herald, Sept. 13, 1881). Others find more difficulty in the subject. One maintains that the character of the contemplated inability must be decided according to the law sense of the term and must, therefore, be an intellectual incapacity of the President, on the happening of which and proof thereof in a manner to be prescribed by the Congress, the office of President devolves on the Vice President (Prof. Dwight, North American Review, Nov., 1881). Another thinks that the Constitution intends to provide for the case of an inability either physical or mental, which is to be known to the Vice President when "so open, notorious, and indisputable as to be recognized by all as existing" (ex-Senator Trumbull, Ibid.). Still another contends that a temporary inability is not contemplated by the provision, but that the inability intended to be provided for depends upon its probable continuance and the condition of public affairs, and that the Congress is to declare when such exists; in other words, that "an inability, in the constitutional sense, is one that not only exists presently, but, in the opinion of Congress, is of such a nature and probable continuance that it causes or threatens inconvenience in public affairs"; on the happening of which, though the President may not again resume his powers, the Vice President is only to act as President, for he can not become President, the elected President still actually living (Judge Cooley, Ibid.). And, again, it is said that any inability, of whatever character and however transient, is what the Constitution aims to provide for; that the Vice President, himself determining when such inability has arisen, shall thereupon enter upon the discharge of the presidential duties; and that when the inability ceases the President is to resume his functions and the Vice President to go back to his place in the Senate (ex-Gov. Butler, Ibid.).

Perhaps the most natural explanation of these varying opinions is to be found in the character of the subject and its mode of treatment, above suggested; it is practically res integra, than which nothing is more inviting, and at the same time stimulating, to the human mind; and it has been dealt with from the point of view of the language of the provision. Did the solution of the problem depend upon "authority" and the citation of precedents, diverse enough would be the conclusions reached; and independence of authority and precedent, setting the matter at large, does not conduce to lessen the number of such conclusions or to promise for them any nearer approach to similarity.

But another explanation suggests itself, to be found in the constitutional nature of the provision; accounting as well for the simplicity of its statement and the different conceptions of its scope and meaning, as for the comparative absence of resort to authority or precedent in its consideration; not that much light may not be thrown on the inquiry by study of the origin and development of the provision, but the case almost wholly wants those direct declarations of intent and expressions of opinion which may be brought forward in almost every other constitutional discussion. The provision in question is matter of detail purely; no principle is involved in it, and the debates of the Federal convention, as also the States in considering the Constitution, show an absence of any discussion of it whatever. Referred to it is, as a matter of course, but only by the way, not to be dwelt upon or even stated in an argumentative or explanatory way, and of the many amendments proposed by one State or another, no one makes any reference to the subject. The nearest approach to notice of the question of inability to be found in the debates is the amendment proposed by New York: "That all commissions * * * shall * * * be tested in the name of the President of the United States, or the person holding his place for the time being" (2 Deb., 408). But this is far from touching the questions in respect of which the provision is here under consideration; those, namely, above stated: What constitutes an inability, who shall decide its existence, and what is the proper course of action on its happening and cessation.

But this apparent want of attention to the provision should not be misconceived; nor should it be overstated or misstated, as, from imperfect consideration of the subject, it not infrequently has been. Thus it has been repeatedly said that the provision for a Vice President was conceived in the closing days of the Federal Convention, when it was not possible to give the subject deserved attention; which statement, while apparently founded in fact, rests on a complete misconception. It is true that, in respect of succession to the powers and duties of the Presidency, the Vice President was provided for at that late day; but he was conceived merely as a substitute in that behalf for the President of the Senate for whom, as contemplated successor to those powers and duties, provision had been made from the first.

Again, so experienced a statesman as ex-Senator Trumbull has used these words: "The original Constitution did not prescribe the qualifications of age and citizenship of Vice President as it did of President. Hence a Vice President not eligible to the Presidency might, under the Constitution as it existed prior to 1804, have had devolved upon him the powers and duties of the presidential office" (N. Amer. Rev., Nov., 1881, p. 419). And in debate in the Senate on January 8, 1883, Senator Dawes held language to the same effect: "So little considered was the provision in reference to the Vice President that they did not even provide that the Vice President should have the qualifications for office that the President should have" (Cong. Rec., vol. 14, No. 29, p. 10). But a glance at Article II, section 1, of the Constitution as it originally stood will show that the third paragraph of that section provides for a balloting by every elector for two persons, and a list of all the persons voted for; of whom the person receiving the highest number of votes should be President, and in every case after the choice of the President the person having the next greatest number should be Vice President; and the fifth paragraph prescribes the qualifications for eligibility to the office of President. As the electors in voting could not designate their choice for President and Vice President, respectively, and as either of the two persons voted for by each of them might be chosen President, it followed as of course that the qualifications for eligibility must be had by all the persons voted for, of whom one must be Vice President. Wherefore the qualifications of the Vice President were necessarily prescribed by the method of his election; and those qualifications were the same as in the case of the President.

While, then, the framers of the Constitution were not remiss, yet the provision under consideration apparently did not receive the same attention at their hands as did the other provisions. But neither was this because of carelessness, nor is it strange. It is just what might be expected, considering the object in view.

The main features to be provided for as to the Executive were: First, the character of the office; second, the qualifications of the incumbent; third, the mode of his election; fourth, his powers and duties; fifth, his tenure. Each of these was the fruitful source of earnest, often confused, and at times seemingly hopeless discussion. This was transferred, after the preparation of the Constitution, to the State conventions and there gone over again and again. In all these features the gravest principles were involved; but those principles once settled, there was left to consider only a possible vacancy during the term for which a President might be chosen. This was a matter wholly secondary to the main consideration, that, namely, of providing an executive; and it was disposed of by a provision wholly simple in its language and, doubtless to the minds of the Convention, also in its meaning and operation.

How a vacancy might occur was evident. It might happen by act of God, as death; by act of another branch of Government, as removal; or by act or condition of the incumbent himself. And this last might be either voluntary, as resignation or absence, or involuntary, as inability.

The death of a President is a matter about which no great doubt can exist; and the same is equally true of his removal from office and his resignation, when either is once a fact. But, it may be said, inability may exist as a fact and yet grave doubt of its being a fact exist at the same time. In turn, it may also be said and confidently that the Convention was not blind to this; yet it saw fit to leave the provision in its present shape. The questions, What is an inability? Who shall decide its existence? were put, but not answered or even discussed in the Convention, "What," asked Mr. Dickinson, "is the extent of the term 'disability' (that being the form originally), and who is to be the judge of it?" (5 Deb., 481). Here the whole question was broached, but nothing followed the inquiry; and in the State conventions the inquiry was not even put.

The care with which the Federal Convention worked out every provision incorporated into the Constitution is yet the theme of our wondering praise. Is the provision under consideration an exception in this particular? We must think not, but that the provision was left as it is, not through carelessness, nor because it was not thought probable that in the brief term fixed for the office an inability might occur; for the Constitution would, for either of those reasons, have been wholly silent on the subject. In fact, the Convention thought the provision as adopted self-explanatory, self-operative, and sufficient. Not only do the character of its members and the earnestness of its deliberations compel us to this view, but also especially must the silence on Dickinson's inquiry and its failure to reappear be deemed conclusive of the point. And additional weight is given this view by the amendment proposed by New York, above mentioned; it is inconceivable that that amendment could be suggested and not one providing for determination of the existence of an inability, etc., if the Constitution was thought to leave any doubt on the point.

That this is the real explanation in the premises, and that the provision was in fact not slighted in point of attention, will be made clearer by considering the question from the other point of view, that, namely, of the proceedings of the Convention, and by reviewing its successive steps on the way to the provision; and this consideration will also aid much in arriving at the construction now to be put upon its language.

The first provision touching the Executive was the seventh of Randolph's resolutions, which, when originally offered, on May 29, 1787, was wholly silent on the subject of succession or substitution (1 Deb., 144; 5 do., 128).

The next in order was Charles Pinckney's draft, submitted the same day, Article VIII of which provided in respect of the President that—

He shall be removed from his office on impeachment by the House of Delegates, and conviction, in the Supreme Court, of treason, bribery, or corruption. In case of his removal, death, resignation, or disability, the President of the

Senate shall exercise the duties of his office until another President be chosen. And in case of the death of the President of the Senate, the Speaker of the House of Delegates shall do so (1 Deb. 148; 5 do. 131).

On being read, Pinckney's draft was referred to the committee of the whole (1 Deb. 150).

On June 15 Mr. Patterson submitted his propositions, of which the fourth provided for a plural executive, ineligible for reelection, "and removable on impeachment and conviction for malpractices or neglect of duty by Congress on application by a majority of the executives of the several States" (1 Deb. 176; 5 do. 192); but these propositions also were wholly silent as to succession or substitution of any officer in the President's stead. The propositions, like Pinckney's draft, were at once referred to a Committee of the Whole House (1 Deb. 177).

On June 18 Hamilton, in a speech, presented his plan of government, Article V of which was as follows:

On the death, resignation, or removal of the governor (Hamilton's title for the executive), his authority to be exercised by the President of the Senate until a successor be appointed (1 Deb. 179).

Hamilton's plan contemplated the continuance in office of the executive during good behavior and made no provision for the case of inability (Cf. 5 Deb. 587).

No other general plans were proposed for the consideration of the convention. On May 30 the House resolved itself into a Committee of the Whole to consider the state of the Union, and took up Randolph's resolutions (1 Deb. 150), which furnished the basis of consideration throughout the convention. The resolution respecting the executive was taken up on June 1 (1 Deb. 154), and, on June 2, postponed to the consideration of the resolution respecting the second branch of the legislature (1 Deb. 156).

No definite action on Randolph's seventh resolution had been taken when, on June 19, the committee disagreed to Patterson's propositions, and a second time reported the resolutions of Randolph (1 Deb. 180; Cf. pp. 174–175). While in Committee of the Whole the convention had left Pinckney's draft untouched; and though in Randolph's resolutions as now reported it was provided by that touching the executive (now numbered 9), that the President should "be removable on impeachment and conviction of malpractice or neglect of duty," the resolutions were still silent on the subject of succession or substitution (1 Deb. 182). So the matter of a disability or an inability was still unprovided for.

The executive continued for a long time a stumbling block, and when, on July 23, the proceedings were referred to a committee for the purpose of reporting a Constitution, "what respects the supreme executive" was expressly excepted (1 Deb. 216). On the next day, July 24, the subject of the executive was taken up by the House, but almost immediately again postponed (1 Deb. 217). At the same time, the committee of the whole was discharged from acting on the propositions of Pinckney and Patterson, and the propositions were referred to the committee to whom the proceedings of the convention had already been referred, viz, Rutledge, Randolph, Gorham, Ellsworth, and Wilson (1 Deb. 217–218; 5 do. 357–358, 363).

Finally, on July 26, the resolution respecting the executive, as reported on June 19, was adopted and referred to the committee already provided (1 Deb. 219–220). So this committee now had before it the resolutions of Randolph as altered by the Convention, the draft of Pinckney, and the propositions of Patterson (1 Deb. 221; 5 do. 363, 374–376).

The Convention adjourned from July 26 to August 6, during the interval between which dates the committee did its work. We have no record of its proceedings, but when on the latter date it reported to the House the draft prepared by it, the article respecting the President (Art. X) contained, in section 2, the following:

He shall be removed from his office on impeachment by the House of Representatives, and conviction in the Supreme Court, of treason, bribery, or corruption. In case of his removal as aforesaid, death, resignation, or disability to discharge the powers and duties of his office, the President of the Senate shall discharge those powers and duties until another President of the United States be chosen, or until the disability of the President be removed (1 Deb., 228; 5 do., 380).

The draft reported by the committee was then taken up and considered from day to day in Committee of the Whole. Article X was not reached until August 24 (1 Deb., 262), and on August 27, the last clause of that article being reached, its consideration was postponed (1 Deb., 267). On

August 31 such portions of the draft as had been postponed, including this clause, were referred to a committee of a Member from each State, 11 in number (1 Deb., 280). This committee reported September 4, and in their report occur for the first time provisions respecting a Vice President, as distinguished from the President of the Senate. Among these was the following:

The Vice President shall be, ex officio, President of the Senate except when they sit to try the impeachment of the President, in which case the Chief Justice shall preside, and excepting, also, when he shall exercise the powers and duties of President, in which case, and in case of his absence, the Senate shall choose a President pro tempore (1 Deb., 284; 5 do., 507).

And the committee recommended the following as the latter part of the second section of Article X:

(The President) shall be removed from his office, on impeachment by the House of Representatives and conviction by the Senate, for treason or bribery; and, in case of his removal as aforesaid, death, absence, resignation, or inability to discharge the powers and duties of his office, the Vice President shall exercise those powers and duties until another President be chosen or until the inability of the President be removed. (Ibid.)

On September 7 that portion of the committee's report touching the election of President and Vice President was amended by adopting the following:

The Legislature may declare by law what officer of the United States shall act as President in case of the death, resignation, or disability of the President and Vice President, and such officer shall act accordingly until such disability be removed or a President shall be elected (1 Deb., 291; 5 do, 220–221).

On the following day the last clause of section 2, Article X, as reported by the committee (supra) was agreed to (1 Deb., 294), and a committee of five, viz, Johnston, Hamilton, G. Morris, Madison, and King, appointed "to revise the style of and arrange the articles agreed to by the House" (1 Deb., 295; 5 do, 530). To this committee went the provisions touching inability in the shape in which they are last above given; that is to say, in terms prescribing that in case of inability the Vice President or other officer of the United States exercising the powers and duties of President (or acting as President) should do so until such inability were removed.

The committee reported September 12; the clause providing for the case of removal, etc., as reported being, according to the Journal, as follows:

In case of the removal of the President from office, or of his death, resignation, or inability to discharge the powers and duties of the said office, the same shall devolve on the Vice President, and the Congress may by law provide for the case of removal, death, resignation, or inability both of the President and Vice President, declaring what officer shall then act as President; and such officer shall act accordingly until the disability be removed or the period for choosing another President arrive (1 Deb., 302).

On September 15 this clause was amended by striking out the words "the period for choosing another President arrive" and inserting in place thereof the words "a President shall be elected" (1 Deb., 313). As thus amended the clause was written into the final draft of the Constitution, with this difference, according to Madison's Minutes: Instead of the two semicolons were two commas (5 Deb., 562), although in the Constitution as now frequently printed the semicolons appear (e. g., see Porter's Outlines U. S. Const. Hist., 81).

In view of the stress which has been laid on these semicolons by some in discussing the provision (who could not, however, have examined the clause as it stands in the Revised Statutes, for there the commas are found and not the semicolons), this difference in the punctuation is of no slight significance; and Mr. Madison's form is entitled to be deemed correct, in preference to the other, not only because he found frequent occasion to note errors in the printed journal (in 17 instances at least, of which samples may be found at 5 Deb. 506, 543), but also, and especially, because he was himself a member of the committee on style which prepared the last draft submitted to the Convention. He says specifically that the copy given by him is the copy "as signed," himself italicizing the words (5 Deb. 536), and though the Convention compared "the report from the committee of revision with the articles which were agreed to by the House, and to them referred for arrangement" (the comparison being made paragraph by paragraph), "no entry of the corrections and amendments adopted or proposed appears upon the journals," resort being had to the written interlineations, Mr. Madison's minutes, and the tally sheets to complete the journal (1 Deb. 307).

The exact effect of the committee's action in the premises may be perfectly seen from the following arrangement, side by side, of the clauses as they were adopted by the Convention and their consolidation as effected by the committee:

In case of (the President's) removal as aforesaid, death, absence, resignation, or inability to discharge the powers or duties of his office, the Vice President shall exercise those powers and duties until another President be chosen, or until the inability of the President be removed.

The Legislature may declare by law what officer of the United States shall act as President, in case of the death, resignation or disability of the President and Vice President; and such officer shall act accordingly, until such disability be removed, or a President shall be elected.

In case of the removal of the President from office, or of his death, resignation, or inability to discharge the powers and duties of the said office, the same shall devolve on the Vice President; and the Congress may by law provide for the case of removal, death, resignation, or inability, both of the President and Vice President, declaring what officer shall then act as President; and such officer shall act accordingly, until the disability be removed, or (the period for choosing another President arrive) a President shall be elected.

However much the outcome of the committee's efforts may cause us to doubt its qualifications in respect of style, this chronological examination of the Convention's proceedings in the premises would seem to make clear several things:

1. The Vice President was not, as some have thought, intended to sit in the Senate and act as president at the same time. Even the language of Article I, section 3, as it now stands, manifests this. ("The Senate shall choose their other officers, and also a president pro tempore in the absence of the Vice President, or when he shall exercise the office of President of the United States.")

2. When the provision under consideration left the hands of the Convention, to be put into shape by the committee on style and arrangement, it was distinctly provided that, in case of an inability of the President, the Vice President was not to become President, but to exercise the powers and duties of the President, which exercise was to cease with the inability of the President.

3. The officer intended to be designated by the Congress

in case of the double inability was an officer of the United States.

4. The committee on style and arrangement regarded itself as merely bringing together and combining into one, without alteration of sense or intent, two cognate provisions found lying apart, by each of which provisions exercise of the presidential duties by a substitute was restricted to the period of actual inability. The committee had no authority to alter or amend; no objection was taken to their union of these provisions, which fact indicates that the revised form was not regarded as in any particular altering or amending "the articles agreed to by the House"; and Mr. Madison's punctuation (which is that actually adopted) makes the clause "until the disability be removed" part of a continuous sentence and therefore constructively, if not strictly, referable alike to the case of the Vice President and the "officer" to be designated by the Congress. And this is a complete answer to Prof. Dwight's assertion that "the specific reference to powers and duties was deliberately rejected, as well as the words 'until the disability be removed,'" so far as that assertion intends to imply that the new form imports alteration or amendment of the Convention's determinations.

These conclusions are not in any sense antagonized by the language of the provision as we now find it. The language is, "in case of * * * inability to discharge the powers and duties of the said office, the same shall devolve on the Vice President." "The same" has reference to the object of the verb "discharge," which is not "said office," for that is the object of the preposition "of," but "the powers and duties of the said office": and the expression "in case of inability" may fairly be construed as equivalent to "during an inability," which would involve return of the executive duties to the President on cessation of the inability.

Nor are Prof. Dwight's citations from Munroe and Martin inconsistent with this view. Munroe was objecting to the Vice President as an unnecessary officer and noting his dangerous influence from the standpoint of "advantage to the State he comes from" (3 Deb., 489–490). "He is," said Munroe, "to succeed the President in case of removal, disability, etc., and to have the casting vote in the Senate." In the connection in which Prof. Dwight cites the former part of this remark the word "succeed," as used by Munroe, is absolutely colorless. The same remark is applicable to the extract from Martin's letter. Martin was writing in almost the identical vein in which Munroe spoke, and in stating his objections to the Vice President he spoke of him as the officer "to supply (the President's) place" (1 Deb., 378). In neither instance was the question of inability under consideration; each used the quoted expression in the run of argument and by way of recital of features deemed objectionable. It would be as fair to cite against Prof. Dwight's contention that the "office" devolves Madison's assertion (in the same debate in which Munroe was arguing) that "the power will devolve on the Vice President" (3 Deb., 498); notwithstanding the remark, being made by Madison while arguing in favor of the provision touching the Executive, has no sort of reference to the point of view from which the provision is now being considered. Indeed, Madison might more justly be cited, for his exact language was, "(the House of Representatives) can impeach (the President) ; they can remove him if found guilty; they can suspend him when suspected, and the power will devolve on the Vice President." But such remarks, made in such connections, are no more to the point than are the dicta of judges' law.

Reverting now, with the aid of this review of the Convention's proceedings, to the several views of the meaning and intent of the provision above noticed, that taken by ex-Gov. Butler would seem to be the correct one. He thinks that the inability may be of any kind, and that when it ceases both officers, President and Vice President, should return to their proper places. The "articles as agreed to by the House" incontestably manifest this, and "this view is in consonance with the whole theory of an alternative officer in all parliamentary bodies and in executive offices" (North Amer. Rev., Nov., 1881, p. 434).

And the Vice President is the person to decide when the inability has arisen. In the absence of any designation to the contrary, "it may be taken to be axiomatic that when the Constitution imposes a duty on an officer, to be done by him, he must be the sole judge when and how to do that duty, subject only to his responsibility to the people and to the risk of impeachment if he act improperly or corruptly" (ibid, 433); a remark which gains weight from consideration of the complete isolation respectively of the executive, judicial, and legislative branches of our Governmeent; than which no feature of our system was more in contemplation by its framers or has been more rigidly respected. The best judgments now agree even that the Supreme Court can not (except by mandamus in those cases of nonfeasance wholly independent of discretion), lay down law for the Executive; the function of that court being only to decide "cases arising" under the prescribed conditions. And the legislature can interfere with the Executive only by impeachment for malfeasance of a specific sort, so that neither the judiciary nor the legislature being either capable of affecting or responsible for the performance of the executive duties, the discharge of those duties is properly left where the responsibility belongs.

Of course, save in the exceptional case of an insane President, no Vice President would assume to insist to a President against his judgment that he was under an inability; and so long as a sane President would resist such intimation there would be no inability. The President may safely be trusted to help out the Vice President in the necessity of deciding to assume the functions of the office, save only in the case of insanity, as suggested; but the Constitution could not go into every exceptional case. Section 675 of the Revised Statutes provides that "in case of a vacancy in the office of Chief Justice, or of his inability to perform the duties and powers of his office, they shall devolve upon the associate justice who is first in precedence." What is an inability in this case, and who decides it? Section 10 of the act of March 1, 1792 (1 Stat., 239; R. S., sec. 147) provides "that whenever the office of President and Vice President shall both become vacant the Secretary of State shall forthwith cause a notification thereof to be made to the executive of every State." Who decides when the two offices are vacant? In the one case the senior associate takes the seat of the Chief Justice because the latter is not in it, and in the other the Secretary of State, being charged with the duty, would discharge it when he himself deemed the occasion to have arisen. And, as Senator Ingalls said in the debate of January 8, 1883, already noticed, "By the Constitution itself, if the Constitution is self-operative or could be self-operative, the powers and duties of (the presidential) office did devolve upon Vice President Arthur on the 2d day of July, 1881."

The determination of the question of inability is an Executive affair altogether. The only other power said to be concerned in it is the Congress, but that body is under a limitation in the premises confining its participation to quite another matter. The Constiution has provided that when an inability exists in one case the Vice President shall act, and that the Congress may—do what? Determine when an inability has arisen in any case? No; but provide what officer shall act when such inability exists in another case. This merely gives the Congress the right to designate an officer to succeed to the discharge of the Executive duties when the double disability exists; it does not even give that body the right to say under what circumstances such disability shall be deemed to have arisen, much less to determine when a wholly different disability occurs. Inclusio unius exclusio alterius; and the Congress recognized this by the act of 1792, which act is a distinct interpretation by that body of its constiutional rights and duties in the premises. That interpretation is perfectly expressed by the language of Senator Morgan (Dec. 29, 1882): "Whenever we proceed further than to declare what officer shall act as President, we transgress the bounds of our constitutional authority."

And immediately in this connection there at once presents itself a question, which, even without its answer, not only indicates that the Constitution did not intend to vest the Congress with the power to determine when or under what circumstances an inabilty exists, but also suggests the reason for the shape in which we find that subject left by the Constitution: How could the Congress decide an inability to exist? Only in one of two ways: First, by special decision in each case as it arises; or, second, by a general provision prescribing a method in advance or conferring the power of decision upon some person or body, to be exercised in a prescribed manner and under prescribed conditions.

It may safely be said that the first of these methods needs no serious consideration. All that is urged against the power of the Congress to interfere at all in the determining the existence of an inability applies with more than double force to its interference without previous provision therefor, and the difficulties in the way of its acting at all in such case are apparent. The alleged or possible existence of an inability is a matter calling for instant consideration and decision, not a matter to be left to the consideration, discussion, perhaps wrangling, of a great number of variously disposed and diverse-minded men. Besides, suppose an inability to appear during a recess of the Congress, what is to be the proceeding?

And here is presented still another important consideration. The very fact that the Constitution contains no provision for summoning the Congress by any other than the
President is almost proof conclusive that that branch was
intended to have no part in determining the existence of
an inability; for to say that the Vice President might so summon that body is to yield the whole question; the very act
by the Vice President would determine the inability to
exist. If provision were made or to be made for summoning the Congress by any other than the President to consider a supposed disability how would the body be summoned? Clearly some one person would be compelled to
take the initiative; and how delicate would be his task, practically deciding the question in advance. Would such task
be much less delicate than that of the Vice President assuming to declare an inability to exist and acting accordingly? And whom could the Congress choose so agreeable to
the people as the second man in power, he who was dis-
tinctively put into his place to assume its great responsibilities?

Putting aside the constitutional objection, the second
method of action by the Congress would be little, if any,
more feasible or satisfactory than the first; and if the Congress should assume to regulate the subject at all, this
second method, delegating power to a person or body, would
be indispensable to provide for the case of an inability
occurring during a recess.

If the Congress should confer the power of decision upon
any one person the matter would be left just where the Constitution leaves it; with this difference in favor of the Constitution—save in the rare instance of the want of a Vice
President, that instrument (if the view herein contended for
be the proper one), confers the power upon one elected to
his office by the people. On the other hand, if the power
were committed to a body, the initiative would necessarily
be taken by some one person; in any aspect of the matter,
the necessity of beginning with some one person constantly
meets us.

Is not this fact practically the explanation of the whole
matter as we find it in the Constitution? The beginning, in
every conceivable view of the case, must always be by some
individual; whether the Vice President is to decide of himself, whether the Congress is to be called, whether any given
person is to exercise the power or any designated body is to

be convened for the purpose, that necessity can not be escaped. And why not leave the matter to the man chosen of the people as their possible ruler? nay, as the Constitution then stood, to the man possibly to be chosen as their ruler; for any one of the men voted for by the electors might be President, and some one of those voted for as President would be the Vice President.

The decision of such a question as the existence of an inability must be prompt and immediately effective; of all questions in the world this should be free from everything approaching delay or halting. There should in such case be no interregnum, be it of how short duration soever; a thing abhorred of all and repugnant to every system of government. A plural tribunal of any sort would involve danger of this great evil, and it needs no inspiration to conceive circumstances under which, with a tribunal of several to consider it, an inability of the President would be almost as great a calamity as an outbreak of treasonable hostilities. A single mind is the best conceivable tribunal for such a question and that tribunal may safely enough be the mind of him who is practically the choice of the whole people. For his right doing in so trying an emergency the Constitution rests its hope, as our entire governmental system rests its life, upon the earnest and patriotic intelligence of the American people and of each and every of them. He would be a rare man, indeed, who, in so responsible a moment, should misconceive, or, worse still, should intentionally disregard his high duty and the inconcealable public sentiment.

Appendix II

Disability Clauses in Colonial Charters

The charters were usually granted to a person or persons and their "heires, deputyes, agents, commissioners and assigns." So executive power in early America transferred automatically by *descent*. As democracy grew, the lieutenant governor emerged as a "deputie" rather than "heire." Pertinent sections of the charters and constitutions of the thirteen Colonies and the states of the Confederation follow: All page citations are to Francis N. Thorpe, *American Charters, Constitutions and Organic Laws* (Washington: Government Printing Office, 1909). Emphasis supplied.

CONNECTICUT:

Council for New England, 1620: "unto which President, *or in his Absence,* to any such Person as by the Order of said Councill shall be thereunto appointed, Wee do give Authority to give Orders. . . ." p. 1831.

Commission to Andros, 1688: "and upon your death or absence out of our said Territory unto our Leut. Governor, to whom we do therefore by these presents give and grant all and singular the powers and authorityes aforesaid to be exercised and enjoyed by him in case of your death or absence *during "our pleasure, or untill your arrival* within our said Territory and Dominion; as Wee do further hereby give and grant full power and authority to our Leut. Governor to do and execute whatsoever he shall be by you authorized and appointed to do and execute in pursuance of and according to the powers grante to you by this Commission." p. 1869.

Government of New Haven Colony, 1643: "the Governor, *or in his absence,* the Deputy Governor, *shall have power* to summon a Generall Court at any other time." p. 528.

Charter of Connecticut, 1662: "That the Governor of the said Company for the Time being, or *in his Absence by occasion of sickness,* or otherwise by his Leave or Permission, the Deputy Governor, for the Time being, shall and may from time to Time upon all Occasions give Order for the assembling of the said Company, and calling them together to consult and advise of the Business and Affairs of the said Company. . . ." p. 531.

DELAWARE:

Dutch West India Company's Patent, 1621: "governor in chief, as well as other deputy governors. . . ." p. 60.

Grant to William Penn, 1681: "Governor, or his Deputy." p. 3045.

Frames of Government, 1682: Notice of council meeting to be given by "the Governor or his Deputy" and ". . . in this provincial Council the Governor *or his Deputy*, shall or may, always preside. . . ." p. 3055.

Constitution of 1776: "And on his [the president's] death, *inability, or absence from the State*, the speaker of the house of assembly *shall have the powers of* a president, until a new nomination is made by the general assembly." p. 563.

GEORGIA:

Proprietary Proposals, 1663: "the Governor or his Deputy to be one, to govern for the time aforesaid. . . ." p. 2754.

Fundamental Constitutions, Carolina, 1669: "One The eldest of the lords proprietors shall be palatine; and upon the decease of the palatine, the eldest of the seven surviving proprietors shall always succeed him. . . . The palatine shall. . . . have power . . . to make a deputy, who *shall have the same power* to all intents and purposes as he himself who deputizes him. . . ." pp. 2772, 2779.

Constitution of Georgia, 1777: "Article XXIX. The president of the executive council, *in the absence or sickness of the governor,* shall exercise all *the powers* of the governor." p. 777.

MARYLAND:

Constitution of Maryland, 1776: XXXII. That upon the death, resignation, or removal out of this State, of the Governor, the first named of the Council, "for the time being, *shall act as Governor,* and qualify in the same manner; and shall immediately call a meeting of the General Assembly, giving not less than fourteen days notice of the meeting, at which meeting, a Governor shall be appointed, in manner aforesaid, for the residue of the year." p. 1686.

MASSACHUSETTS:

Charter of Massachusetts Bay, 1629: "There shalbe one Governor, one Deputy Governor . . . That the Governor of the saide Company for the tyme being, *or in his Absence by Occasion of Sicknes or otherwise,* the Deputie Governor for the tyme being, *shall have Authoritie* from time to time upon all Occasions, to give order for the assembling of the saide Company. . . . (etc.)" p. 1852.

Charter of Massachusetts Bay, 1691: ". . . there shall be one Governour One Leivtent or Deputy Governour . . . when and as often as the Governour "of our said Province for the time being shall happen to dye or be displaced by us . . . or be absent from his Government That then and in any of the said Cases the Lievtenant or Deputy Governour of Our said Province for the time being shall have full power and authority to doe and execute all and every suc Acts Matters and things which our Governour of Our said Province for the time being might or could by vertue of these Our Letters Patents lawfully doe or execute if he were personally present *untill the returne of the Governour soe absent or Arrivall or Constitucon of such other Governour as shall or may be appointed. . . .*" pp. 1877, 1884.

Constitution of Massachusetts, 1780: "Whenever the chair of the governor shall be vacant, by reason of his death, or absence from the commonwealth, *or otherwise,* the lieutenant-governor, for the time being, shall, during such vacancy, *perform all the duties* incumbent upon the governor, and shall have and *exercise all the powers and authorities,* which by this "constitution the governor is vested with, when personally present." p. 1888.

NEW HAMPSHIRE:

Constitution of 1776: "that such Council appoint their President, and in his absence that the senior counsellor preside." p. 2451.

Constitution of 1784: "Whenever the chair of the president shall be vacant, by reason of death, absence for the state, *or otherwise,* the senior senator for the time being, shall, during such vacancy, have and *exercise all the powers and authorities* which by this constitution the president is vested with when personally present." p. 2453.

NEW JERSEY:

Constitution of 1776: The Council shall choose a "Vice President, *who shall act as such* in the absence of the Governor." p. 2596.

NEW YORK:

Constitution of 1777: "And in the case of the impeachment of the governor, or his removal from office, death, resignation, or absence from the State, the lieutenant governor *shall exercise all the power and authority* appertaining to the office of the governor until another be chosen, or the governor absent or impeached shall return or be acquitted. . . ."

NORTH CAROLINA:

Constitution of 1776: ". . . And on his death, *inability,* or absence from the State, the Speaker of the Senate, for the time being (and in case of this death, inability, or absence from the State, the Speaker of the House of Commons) shall *exercise the powers* of government after such death, or during such absence or inability of the Governor (or Speaker of the Senate) or until a new nomination is made by the General Assembly." p. 2792.

PENNSYLVANIA:

Constitution of 1776: "The president, *and in his absence,* the vice president with the council" shall *exercise* the executive power. p. 3087.

See also comment under DELAWARE concerning the 1681 grant to William Penn, and the Frames of Government of 1682.

RHODE ISLAND:

Charter of Rhode Island and Providence Plantations, 1663: "there shall bee one Governour, one Deputie-Governour and ten Assistants . . . the Governour of the sayd Company, for the tyme being, or in his absence, *by occasion of sicknesse, or otherwise,* by his leave and permission, the Deputy-Governour for the tyme being shall and may, from tyme to tyme, upon all occasions, give order for the assemblyings of the sayd Company. ... (etc.)" p. 3214.

SOUTH CAROLINA:

See the Fundamental Constitutions, Carolina, 1669 under GEORGIA.

Constitution of 1776: "That in the case of the death of the president and commander-in-chief, or his absence from the colony, the vice-president of the colony shall *succeed to his office....*" p. 3245.

Constitution of 1778: "That in case of the impeachment of the governor and commander-in-chief, or his removal from office, death, resignation, or absence from the state, the lieutenant governor shall *succeed to his office.*" p. 3249.

VIRGINIA:

Constitution of 1776: "The Privy Council . . . shall annually choose, out of their own members, a President, who, in case of death, *inability*, or absence of the Governor from the Government, *shall act as Lieutenant-Governor.*" p. 3817.

Amendment Proposed by the *Nebraska Law Review*

Article——

Section 1. If the President dies, resigns or is removed from office, the Vice President shall become President for the remainder of the term to which the President was elected.

Section 2. If the President becomes unable for any reason to discharge the powers and duties of his office, they shall devolve upon the Vice President, who shall then act as President until the disability of the President be removed, or the term of office of the President shall expire. Congress shall have the power to establish a procedure to determine the inability of the President to discharge the powers and duties of his office; but such procedure must be compatible with the maintenance of the three distinct departments of government, the legislative, the executive and the judicial and the preservation of the checks and balances between the coordinate branches. Congress shall provide by law for the case of the removal, death, resignation or inability of both the President and Vice President, declaring what officer shall then act as President; and such officer shall act accordingly, until the inability be removed, or the expiration of the term for which both officers had been elected.

Section 3. Article II, section 1, paragraph 6 is hereby repealed.

Appendix IV

American Bar Association

Resolution Adopted by the House of Delegates, February 22, 1960

Resolved, That the American Bar Association approves the adoption of an amendment to the Constitution of the United States on the subject of presidential inability, whereby the fifth clause of Section 1 of Article II of the Constitution would be amended to read as follows:

"In case of the removal of the President from office, or his death or resignation, the said office shall devolve on the Vice President. In case of the inability of the President to discharge the powers and duties of the said office, the said powers and duties shall devolve on the Vice President, until the inability be removed. The Congress may by law provide for the case of removal, death, resignation or inability, both of the President and Vice President, declaring what officer shall then be President, or in the case of inability, act as President, and such officer shall be or act as President accordingly, until a President shall be elected or, in case of inability, until the inability shall be earlier removed. The commencement and termination of any inability shall be determined by such method as Congress shall by law provide."

Amendments with virtually identical wording were subsequently adopted by the New York State Bar Association and the Association of the Bar of the City of New York.

Appendix V

A. Former President Hoover's Suggestions on a Method of Determining Inability

THE KEY LARGO ANGLERS CLUB
Homestead, Fla., January 20, 1958

Hon. Estes Kefauver,
Chairman, Standing Subcommittee on Constitutional Amendments, United States Senate, Washington, D. C.

MY DEAR SENATOR: I have received your kind note requesting my views on the proposed bills you send me.

I assume that the question is solely the method of determining the "inability" of the President "to discharge the powers and duties of his office," and contained in it also the method of determining the "removal of disability."

All questions of succession seem covered by article II, section 1, paragraph 5 of the Constitution, and therefore legislation on this subject seems to me unnecessary.

1. There seems to be some question as to whether remedy can be found by statutory law or must be through constitutional amendment. The Congress will need decide whether the above-mentioned section in the Constitution would be sufficient authority for a statutory solution.

2. It seems to me that the method of determining "inability" or "recovery" requires consideration of the spirit of the separation of powers in the Government and certain traditional practices which have become fixed in our national life during the past 150 years.

3. The President and the Vice President are elected as the chosen leaders of a political party with declared mandates, principles, solutions of issues, and promises to the people.

4. The Congress, in one or both Houses, is often controlled by an opposition political party, and thus by those who are, in practice, mostly opposed to the mandates or promises upon which the President and Vice President are elected by the people.

5. All of which leads me to the generalization that a President's inability to serve or his possible restoration to office should be determined by the leading officials in the executive branch, as they are of the party having the responsibilities determined by the election.

161

6. I believe that a simple amendment to the Constitution (or possibly statutory law) could provide for a commission made up from the executive branch to make the determinations required. I do not suggest that the individual persons be named but that the departments or agencies be enumerated, whose chief official or head should be a member of such a commission. The number could well be limited to not less than 7 and not more than 15 such heads of departments or agencies. There could be a further provision that they should seek the advice of a panel of experienced physicians or surgeons.

I cannot conceive of any circumstance when such a defined body of leaders from the executive branch would act in these circumstances otherwise than in the national interest.

Yours faithfully,

(Signed) HERBERT HOOVER

B. Former President Truman's Proposal

INDEPENDENCE, MO.

January 16, 1958

Hon. Estes Kefauver,
    United States Senate,
    Washington, D. C.

DEAR ESTES: In reply to your letter of the 10th, I am sending you a copy of an article of mine, written for the North American Newspaper Alliance, which covers the subject of a President's inability to carry on his duties.

These are my views, and if you want to make use of the article, you are at liberty to do so.

Sincerely yours,

(Signed) HARRY TRUMAN

(Copyright by Harry S. Truman, 1957)

There has been an understandable reluctance to deal with the delicate and sensitive problem of what we are to do when any President becomes incapacitated and is unable to perform his duties.

Our Founding Fathers did not provide for such an eventuality. During the 168 years of our history under the

Constitution, there have been only two occasions when the question arose of a President's ability to serve. I refer to James A. Garfield and Woodrow Wilson. We have been fortunate, indeed, that we have not had to face such a crisis more often.

But the job of the President is getting to be an almost unendurable mental and physical burden, and we ought not to go on trusting to luck to see us through.

We may find that we have waited too long to provide a way of meeting the situation in the event a President becomes incapacitated. There have been suggestions to deal with the matter through legislation. Others have proposed amending the Constitution.

However we deal with it eventually, this is too vital a matter to be acted on hastily without the widest discussion and study. I have felt that there is always great danger in writing too much into the Constitution. We must have certain flexibility to meet changing conditions. We have already experienced the consequences of hastily amending the Constitution without adequate public discussion, as in the cases of the 18th and the 22d amendments.

In response to the many letters I have received on the subject from all parts of the country, and the world, I am taking the liberty of suggesting a way to meet this problem.

I would like to make it perfectly clear that it is not my intention to cast reflections on anyone, or to raise any doubts about the health or condition of the President. Along with all of our citizens, I wish him good health and a long life.

But there is a growing concern about our needs to provide against the danger of a lapse in the functioning of the Presidency and the crises that might ensue.

The power of the President of the United States and his influence on the world today have grown so great that his well-being is of paramount interest to people everywhere. It is no longer a matter to be decided by political leaders and constitutional authority.

Even a minor indisposition of the President will set into motion unexpected and often unreasoning fears, such as we have recently witnessed.

The framers of our Constitution drafted a brilliant and inspired document in which they anticipated and provided for nearly all of the basic developments of our democracy.

But who could fully foresee the role of the American Presidency in the kind of a world in which we now live—a role which also requires the President to be available in person at any hour to make decisions which he alone can make and which cannot be put off?

As Vice President, I found myself acutely conscious of this problem in a personal way when I met President Roosevelt upon his return from Yalta. Up to that time I regarded the circumstances of an incapacitated President as an academic problem in history, such as was posed by Presidents Garfield and Wilson.

After the first shock of seeing President Roosevelt, I tried to dismiss from my mind the ominous thoughts of a possible breakdown, counting on his ability to bounce back from the strains and stress of office. After Yalta, President Roosevelt continued to carry on with sustained energy and alertness—until suddenly called by death.

From the day I succeeded to the Presidency, I have been thinking about the needs of an act of legislation to provide machinery to meet the emergency of a President's disability.

Shortly after taking office, I considered setting up a commission to study the problem and make recommendations. But in the midst of war and during the period of postwar reconstruction we were preoccupied with more immediate and urgent matters.

I therefore chose instead to recommend to the Congress a change by statute of succession to the Presidency from the Cabinet to the Congress in the event the Nation was without a Vice President. Up to that time the Secretary of State was next in order of succession. I did not think that a Cabinet officer—who is not elected by the people—should succeed to the Presidency, which is an elective office. The Speaker of the House, who is, in fact, the top-ranking elected public official after the President and the Vice President, is now under the new law next in succession.

This, however, does not meet the problem when a President is unable to perform the duties of his office.

I suggest, therefore, that the following proposal may provide us with a workable solution:

1. When a President is stricken with an illness, raising the question of his ability to carry out the duties of his office, there should come into being a Committee of Seven composed of representatives of the three branches of the

Government. This Committee should consist of the Vice President, the Chief Justice of the United States, the Speaker of the House, and the majority and minority leaders of both the House of Representatives and the Senate. This Committee would select a board of leading medical authorities drawn from top medical schools of the Nation. This medical board, thus chosen, would then make the necessary examinations presenting their findings to the Committee of Seven. Should the findings of the medical board indicate that the President is unable to perform his duties, and that he is, in fact, truly incapacitated and not merely stricken with a transitory illness, then the Committee of Seven would so inform the Congress. Congress then would have the right to act, and by a two-thirds vote of the full membership declare the Vice President as President.

The Vice President, designated as President, would thereupon serve out the full term of his predecessor. Should the stricken President, thus relieved, experience during this term a complete recovery, he would not be entitled to repossess the office.

Should the Congress be in adjournment or recess when a President is incapacitated, the Vice President, the Speaker, and Chief Justice should call a meeting of the Committee of Seven. This Committee, after receiving the medical findings, would have authority to call Congress into special session for the purpose of declaring the Vice President as President.

2. When a Vice President succeeds to the Presidency and leaves the office of the Vice President vacant, the last electoral college should be called into session by the new President for the purpose of selecting and declaring a new Vice President. I would recommend that in every instance where a Vice President succeeds to an unexpired term of a President the electoral college be convened to choose a new Vice President.

By this procedure I think we would be able to ensure the proper continuance of the functioning of the Presidency and, at the same time, protect the Nation's paramount interests through the full exercise of the checks and balances of our free democratic institutions.

I suggest procedure along these broad general lines could be enacted into law by statute. If necessary, these provisions could be framed into a constitutional amendment.

Notes

CHAPTER I

1. Richard M. Nixon, *Six Crises* (New York: Doubleday & Co., Inc., 1962), p. 139. Emphasis added.
2. *Ibid.*, p. 150.
3. Herbert H. Brownell, Jr., "Presidential Disability: The Need for a Constitutional Amendment," *Yale Law Journal*, LXVIII, No. 2 (December, 1958), 189.

CHAPTER II

1. *Baltimore Republican*, March 23, 1840. Despite the name, it was a Democratic newspaper.
2. Richard B. Morris (ed.), *Encyclopedia of American History* (New York: Harper & Bros., 1953), p. 183.
3. James D. Richardson, *Messages and Papers of the Presidents* (Washington: Government Printing Office, 1897), IV, 10.
4. Robert J. Morgan, *A Whig Embattled* (Lincoln: University of Nebraska Press, 1954), p. 7.
5. Hugh Russell Fraser, *Democracy in the Making* (Indianapolis: Bobbs-Merrill Co., 1938), pp. 149–150.
6. Richardson, *Messages and Papers of the Presidents*, IV, 31.
7. The account of Tyler's notification and his return to Washington is derived mostly from Fraser, *Democracy in the Making*, pp. 151–159.
8. Richardson, *Messages and Papers of the Presidents*, IV, 31–32.
9. *Ibid.*, p. 22.
10. For a discussion of the various stories, see Ruth Silva, *Presidential Succession* (Ann Arbor: University of Michigan Press, 1951), pp. 14–17.
11. According to his son, Tyler thought he had become President at the moment of Harrison's death. Lyon G. Tyler, *Letters and Times of the Tylers* (Richmond, Va.: Whittet and Shepherdson, 1885), II, 12.
12. Herbert W. Horwill, *The Usages of the American Constitution* (London: Oxford University Press, 1925), pp. 70–71.
13. Morgan, *A Whig Embattled*, p. 8. Emphasis added.
14. Silva, *Presidential Succession*, pp. 18–20. Morgan, *A Whig Embattled*, pp. 10–11.
15. Charles Francis Adams (ed.), *Memoirs of John Quincy Adams* (Philadelphia: Lippincott, 1876), X, 463–464.
16. Calvin Colton (ed.), *The Works of Henry Clay* (New York: Putnam's, 1904), II, 355–356.
17. Morgan, *A Whig Embattled*, p. 17.
18. "I don't know if any of you fellows ever had a load of hay or a bull fall on him. . . . But last night the whole weight of the moon and stars fell on me" (Harry S. Truman, quoted in a United Press story, datelined Washington, April 14, 1945).
19. Tyler to Tazewell (October 11, 1841), Lyon G. Tyler, *The Letters and Times of the Tylers*, II, 127.
20. Fraser, *Democracy in the Making*, p. 121.
21. Morgan, *A Whig Embattled*, p. 9.
22. Fraser, *Democracy in the Making*, p. 160.
23. The authoritative work on the Convention was not published until seventy years later: Max Farrand (ed.), *The Records of the Federal Convention* of 1787 (New Haven: Yale University Press, 1911).

24. *Memoirs of John Quincy Adams*, X, 456.

25. Henry E. Davis, *Inability of the President*, Senate Document 308, 65th Cong., 3rd Sess. (1918). See Appendix I.

26. *Ibid.*, p. 10.

27. *Opinions of the Attorneys General*, XLII, No. 5 (August 2, 1961), 9–10.

28. Farrand, *Records of the Federal Convention*, II, 402–403.

29. Charles Warren, *The Making of the Constitution* (Boston: Little Brown and Co., 1928), p. 635.

30. Jonathan Elliot, *The Debates in the Several States* (2nd ed.; Philadelphia: J. B. Lippincott & Co., 1886), II, 85.

31. See also the discussion in Warren, *Making of the Constitution*, p. 673.

32. *Opinions of the Attroneys General*, pp. 13–14.

33. Edward S. Corwin, *The President: Office and Powers* (New York: New York University Press, 1957), p. 54.

34. *Memoirs of John Quincy Adams*, X, 457.

35. Silva, *Presidential Succession*, p. 51.

CHAPTER III

1. Rudolph Marx, M.D., *The Health of the Presidents* (New York: G. P. Putnam's Sons, 1960), pp. 238 ff.

2. Ruth Silva, *Presidential Succession* (Ann Arbor: University of Michigan Press, 1951), pp. 52–53.

3. *Ibid.*, p. 53.

4. Theron Clark Crawford, *James G. Blaine: A Study of His Life and Career* (Philadelphia: J. C. Winston & Co., Inc., 1893), p. 493.

5. Silva, *Presidential Succession*, pp. 54–55.

6. James D. Richardson, *Messages and Papers of the Presidents* (Washington: Government Printing Office, 1897), VIII, 14.

7. *Ibid.*, pp. 65, 147, 187, 235. The dates of the four State of the Union messages were December 6, 1881; December 4, 1882; December 4, 1883; and December 1, 1884.

8. Irving Williams, *The Rise of the Vice Presidency* (New York: Public Affairs Press, 1956), p. 101.

9. A. S. Link, *Wilson: The Road to the White House* (Princeton: Princeton University Press, 1947), pp. 462–463.

10. Ike Hoover, *Forty Years in the White House* (Boston: Houghton Mifflin Co., 1934), pp. 98–99.

11. Joseph P. Tumulty, *Woodrow Wilson as I Knew Him* (Special Edition for the Literary Digest, 1921), p. 434. A trade edition was issued by Doubleday & Co. in 1924.

12. Charles Seymour, "Woodrow Wilson," *Encyclopaedia Britannica*, XXIII (1936), 434. Marx, *The Health of the Presidents*, p. 129.

13. Herbert Hoover, *The Ordeal of Woodrow Wilson* (New York: McGraw-Hill Book Co., 1958), p. 271.

14. Ike Hoover, *Forty Years in the White House*, p. 103. The quotation in the following paragraph is from the same source, p. 106.

15. Edith Bolling Wilson, *My Memoir* (Indianapolis: Bobbs-Merrill, 1938), pp. 228–291. Emphasis added.

16. David F. Houston, *Eight Years with Wilson's Cabinet* (New York: Doubleday & Co., Inc., 1926), II, 36–37.

17. Samuel Flagg Bemis (ed.), *The American Secretaries of State and Their Diplomacy* (New York: Alfred A. Knopf, Inc., 1929), X, 170.

18. Houston, *Eight Years with Wilson's Cabinet*, II, 38–39.

19. Tumulty, *Woodrow Wilson as I Knew Him*, pp. 443–444.

20. Josephus Daniels, *The Life of Woodrow Wilson* (Philadelphia: Universal Book and Bible House, 1924), pp. 150–151.

21. Woodrow Wilson, *Congressional Government* (Boston: Houghton Mifflin Co., 1885), pp. 240–241. Emphasis added.

22. Tumulty, *Woodrow Wilson as I Knew Him*, p. 445.

23. Bemis, *The American Secretaries of State and Their Diplomacy*, X, 170–171.

24. Silva, *Presidential Succession*, p. 61.

25. Marx, *The Health of the Presidents*, p. 321.

26. Thomas R. Marshall, *Recollections of Thomas R. Marshall* (Indianapolis: Bobbs-Merrill Co., *c.* 1925), p. 367.

27. Letters by John Brooks Leavitt to the *New York Times*, December 6, 18, 1921.

28. Josephus Daniels, *The Wilson Era* (Chapel Hill: University of North Carolina Press, 1946), p. 545.

29. Silva, *Presidential Succession*, pp. 57–58.

30. *Ibid.*, p. 60.

31. *Ibid.*, p. 62.

32. *Ibid.*, p. 81.

33. Davis, *Inability of the President*, p. 4.

34. *Ibid.*, p. 7.

35. Corwin, *The President: Office and Powers*, p. 54.

CHAPTER IV

1. Rudolph Marx, *The Health of the Presidents* (New York: G. P. Putnam's Sons, 1960), p. 319.

2. Allan Nevins, *Grover Cleveland: A Study in Courage* (New York: Dodd, Mead & Co., 1948), pp. 528–529. See also Allan Nevins (ed.), *The Letters of Grover Cleveland, 1850–1908* (Boston: Houghton Mifflin Co., 1933), pp. 326, 329, 337.

3. William W. Keen, *The Surgical Operations on President Cleveland in 1893* (Philadelphia: George W. Jacobs & Co., 1917), *passim*. According to Marx, *The Health of the Presidents*, pp. 261–262, a reporter named Edwards, who wrote under the byline of "Holland," gave to "the Philadelphia *Press* a sensational account of the first operation with unusually accurate details that only an insider could have known. The story was vigorously denied by Dr. Bryant. The editor of the Philadelphia *Public Ledger*, L. Clarke Davis, a personal friends of Cleveland, characterized Holland's report as 'an infamous exploitation of a toothache,' and said he had never seen the Chief Executive in better physical or mental condition. Other newspapers also denied that a major operation had been performed. By the time the story came out, the appearance of the President belied it. . . . The sensation aroused throughout the country and the world by Holland's report quickly subsided and was soon forgotten." See also Nevins, *Grover Cleveland*, pp. 532–533.

4. Marx, *The Health of the Presidents*, p. 323. The medical data about President Harding are derived from the same source, pp. 323–336, and from the official bulletins released to the press.

5. Gaston B. Means, *The Strange Death of President Harding* (New York: Guild Publishing Co., 1930).

6. Frances Perkins, *The Roosevelt I Knew* (New York: The Viking Press, 1946), p. 126.

7. Samuel I. Rosenman, *Working with Roosevelt* (New York: Harper & Bros., 1952), pp. 411–412.

8. John Gunther, *Roosevelt in Retrospect* (New York: Harper & Bros., 1950), pp. 371–372. Mr. Gunther notes that the list of alleged ailments is from an article in *Colliers* (March 3, 1945) by George Creel, which is a staunch defense of Dr. McIntire.

9. Robert E. Sherwood, *Roosevelt and Hopkins: An Intimate History* (New York: Harper & Bros., 1948), pp. 820–821, 824.

10. Michael Reilly, *Reilly of the White House* (New York: Simon & Schuster, 1947), pp. 195–196.

11. Elliott Roosevelt, "They're Lying about F.D.R.'s Health," *Liberty*, May, 1949, p. 76.

12. James Roosevelt, *Affectionately, F.D.R.* (New York: Harcourt, Brace & Co., 1959), pp. 350–353, 354–355.

13. Grace Tully, *F.D.R., My Boss* (New York: Charles Scribner's Sons, 1949), p. 351.

14. Harry S. Truman, Article for the North American Newspaper Alliance (1957), cited at Hearings, Senate Subcommittee on Constitutional Amendments, Eighty-fifth Congress, Second Session, p. 12.

15. Edward R. Stettinius, Jr., *Roosevelt and the Russians: The Yalta Conference* (New York: Doubleday & Co., Inc., 1949), pp. 73, 203.

16. Gunther, *Roosevelt in Retrospect*, p. 365.

17. Harry S. Truman, *Memoirs* (Garden City: Doubleday & Co., Inc., 1955), I, 1–3. The quotation in the paragraph which follows is from the same source, p. 5.

18. Karl C. Wold, M.D., "The Truth about F.D.R.'s Health," *Look*, February 15, 1949. The article was taken from Dr. Wold's book, *Mr. President—How Is Your Health?* (Milwaukee: Bruce Publishing Co., 1948), pp. 191–206.

19. Elliott Roosevelt, "They're Lying about F.D.R.'s Health," p. 76.

20. Emmanuel M. Josephson, *The Strange Death of Franklin D. Roosevelt* (New York: Chedney Press, 1948), pp. 282–283.

21. *New York Times*, September 27, 1955, 28:1–6.

22. Quoted in Richard M. Nixon, *Six Crises* (Garden City: Doubleday & Co., Inc., 1962), pp. 137–138.

23. General Eisenhower in a personal interview with Richard H. Hansen, Gettysburg, Pennsylvania, June 29, 1961.

24. Nixon, *Six Crises*, pp. 138–139.

25. *Ibid.*, pp. 142, 146.

26. *Ibid.*, p. 148.

27. Heinlein, "The Problem of Presidential Inability," *University of Cincinnati Law Review*, XXV (1956), 310, quoting *New York Times*, October 2, 1955, p. 1.

28. Sherman Adams, *Firsthand Report* (New York: Harper & Bros., 1961), p. 186.

29. *Ibid.*, pp. 185–186.

30. Nixon, *Six Crises*, p. 150.

31. *Ibid.*, pp. 167–168.

32. Adams, *Firsthand Report*, p. 201.

33. *Ibid.*, p. 196.

34. Nixon, *Six Crises*, p. 171.

35. Adams, *Firsthand Report*, pp. 197–198.

36. Nixon, *Six Crises*, p. 172.

37. *Ibid.*, pp. 173–174.

CHAPTER V

1. Herbert Brownell, Jr., "Presidential Disability: The Need for a Constitutional Amendment," *Yale Law Journal*, Vol. LXVIII, No. 2 (December, 1958).

2. *A. L. A. Schlechter Corp. v. United States*, 295 U. S. 495 (1935).

3. *Hearings, Subcommittee on the Study of Presidential Inability of the House Committee on the Judiciary, United States Senate*, 85th Cong., 2nd Sess. (1958), p. 14.

4. Brownell, "Presidential Disability," p. 199.

5. *Ibid.*, p. 201.

6. Sherman Adams, *Firsthand Report* (New York: Harper & Bros., 1961), p. 201.

7. Statement of Attorney General Rogers on Presidential Inability, App. III, February 18, 1958 (U. S. Dept. of Justice, mimeographed), cited in Brownell, "Presidential Disability," pp. 201–202.

8. Richard M. Nixon, *Six Crises* (New York: Doubleday & Co., Inc., 1962), pp. 178–179.

9. *New York Times*, March 4, 1958, 1:2; 17:1.

10. Brownell, "Presidential Disability," p. 203.

11. Nixon, *Six Crises*, pp. 179–181.

12. *Opinions of the Attorneys General*, XLII, No. 5 (August 2, 1961), p. 1.

13. *Ibid.*, pp. 36–37.

14. *Ibid.*, p. 35.

15. General Dwight D. Eisenhower in a personal interview with Richard H. Hansen, June 29, 1961, Gettysburg, Pa.

16. Murrow and Friendly, *I Can Hear It Now*, Vol. III, 1919–1932, Columbia Records, Inc.

17. Samuel I. Rosenman, *Working with Roosevelt* (New York: Harper & Bros., 1952), p. 487.

18. Josephus Daniels, *The Wilson Era* (Chapel Hill: University of North Carolina Press, 1946), pp. 557–559.

19. Mrs. Ann Whitman, Personal Secretary to General Dwight D. Eisenhower, to Richard H. Hansen, September 6, 1961.

20. 26 Fed. Reg. 9667, 9451, 9375 (1961).

CHAPTER VI

1. *Opinions of the Attorneys General*, XLII, No. 5 (August 2, 1961), 15.

2. Oliver Perry Chitwood, *A History of Colonial America* (New York: Harper & Bros., 1948), pp. 74–77.

3. Pennsylvania Archives, *Governor's Papers, 1681–1747* (Harrisburg: State of Pennsylvania, 1900), 4th Ser., I, 103.

4. Richard H. Hansen, "Executive Disability: A Void in State and Federal Law," *Nebraska Law Review*, XL (1961), 701–703.

5. Alexander Hamilton, *The Federalist*, ed. Henry Cabot Lodge (New York: G. P. Putnam's Sons, 1888), No. LXVIII, p. 427.

6. *Advisory Opinion to Acting Governor Johns,* 67 So. 2d 413 (1953). The following cases all concern succession through death: *State ex rel. Sadler v. La Grave,* 23 Nev. 216, 45 P. 243, 35 L.R.A. 233 (1896); *State ex rel. Hardin v. Sadler,* 23 Nev. 356, 47 P. 450 (1897); *State ex rel. Murphy v. McBride,* 29 Wash. 255, 70 P. 25 (1902); *State ex rel. Concini v. Garvey,* 67 Ariz. 304, 195 P. 2d 153 (1948).

7. *Olcott v. Hoff,* 92 Ore. 462, 181 P. 466 (1919); *State ex rel. Roberts v. Olcott,* 94 Ore. 683, 187 P. 286 (1920); *State ex rel. Chatterton v. Grant,* 12 Wyo. 1, 73 P. 470 (1903).

8. *Opinion of the Judges,* 3 Neb. 463.

9. *People ex rel. Robin v. Hayes,* 163 App. Div. 725, 149 N.Y.S. 250 (1914); *State ex rel. Olson v. Langer,* 65 N. D. 68, 256 N.W. 377 (1934); *Fitzpatrick v. McAlister,* 121 Okla. 83, 248 P. 569 (1926).

10. Donald Day, *Autobiography of Sam Houston* (Norman: University of Oklahoma Press, 1954), p. 47.

11. *People ex rel. Hopkins,* 55 N. Y. 74 (1873).

12. *In re Moore,* 4 Wyo. 98, 31 P. 980 (1892); *State v. Heller,* 63 N. J. 105, 42 Atl. 155 (1899); *People ex rel. Parks v. Cornforth,* 34 Colo. 107, 81 P. 871 (1905); *Futrell v. Oldham,* 107 Ark. 386, 155 S.W. 502 (1913); *State ex rel. Lamey v. Mitchell,* 97 Mont. 252, 34 P. 2d 369 (1934).

13. *Thompson v. Talmadge,* 201 Ga. 867, 41 S.E. 2d 883 (1942).

14. *State ex rel. Cyr v. Long,* 174 La. 169, 140 So. 13 (1932).

15. *Barnard, Attorney General v. Taggart,* 66 N. H. 362, 29 Atl. 1027 (1890).

16. *Ibid.,* 29 Atl. 1027 at 1028.

17. *Ibid.,* 29 Atl. 1027 at 1029.

18. *Ibid.*

19. *Ibid.*

20. Henry E. Davis, *Inability of the President,* Senate Document 308, 65th Cong., 3rd Sess. (1918), p. 13.

21. Herbert Brownell, Jr., "Presidential Disability: The Need for a Constitutional Amendment," *Yale Law Journal,* LXVIII, No. 2 (December, 1958), 204, cited in *Opinions of the Attorney General,* XLII, No. 5 (August 2, 1961), 29.

22. *Wrede v. Richardson,* 82 N.E. 1072 at 1075 (1907).

23. Joseph E. Kallenbach, *Presidential Inability,* House Committee Print, 84th Cong., 2nd Sess. (1956).

24. *Opinion of the Judges,* 87 N. H. 489.

25. A note in the *University of Chicago Law Review,* VIII (1941), 521 discusses the case exhaustively.

26. *World Almanac* (1960), p. 107. Supplemental material is: *Opinion of the Attorney General of Louisiana,* June 22, 1959, p. 195; *Time,* June 29, 1959, p. 13; *Time,* September 19, 1960, p. 25; *Newsweek,* July 13, 1959, p. 19.

27. *Lincoln Evening Journal,* April 18, 1959, 1:7; *Lincoln Star,* April 22, 1959, 1:5 *Lincoln Evening Journal,* April 23, 1959, 1:6 and May 1, 1959, 1:4.

28. *Lincoln Evening Journal,* April 28, 1960, 4:1.

29. *Lincoln Star,* August 24, 1960, 1:2; *Lincoln Evening Journal,* August 30, 1960, 1:1.

30. *Lincoln Star,* September 10, 1960, 1:1.

31. *Ibid.,* September 1, 1960, 38:1.

32. *Laws, Nebraska, 1961,* Ch. 452, p. 1379.

33. *Oregon Revised Statutes,* secs. 176.040, 176.050.

34. *Alabama,* Art. V, sec. 128; *Mississippi,* Art. V, sec. 131; *New Jersey,* Art. 4, sec. 1, para. 8.

35. *Opinions of the Attorney General,* XLII, No. 5 (August 2, 1961), 16. The citation is from Joseph E. Kallenbach, *Presidential Inability,* House Committee Print, 84th Cong. 2nd Sess. (1956), p. 40.

36. *Nebraska Law Review Survey.*

CHAPTER VII

1. Ruth Silva, *Presidential Succession* (Ann Arbor: University of Michigan, 1951), pp. 83–84.

2. *Ibid.,* pp. 84–85.

3. Letter from Merriman Smith to Richard H. Hansen, October 21, 1960.

4. The study was first summarized in *Nebraska Law Review,* XL (1961), 697.

5. Herbert C. Hoover to Richard H. Hansen, March 15, 1962.

6. Herbert Brownell, "Presidential Inability: The Need for a Constitutional Amendment," *Yale Law Journal,* LXVIII, No. 2 (December, 1958), 205.

7. Cornelius W. Wickersham, "Presidential Inability: Procrastination, Apathy and the Constitution," *Villanova Law Review,* VII, 267.

8. Wickersham, "Presidential Inability," pp. 268–269. Emphasis has been added.

9. Harry S. Truman, article for the North American Newspaper Alliance (1957), cited *Hearings, Senate Subcommittee on Constitutional Amendments,* 85th Cong., 2nd Sess. (1958), pp. 11–12.

10. *Opinions of the Attorneys General,* XLII, No. 5 (August 2, 1961), 23–24.

11. *Ibid.,* p. 19.

12. Wickersham, "Presidential Inability," p. 265.

13. *Opinions of the Attorneys General,* XLII, 31–32.

14. See note 9 *supra.*

15. *Chadwick v. Earhart,* 11 Oregon 389 at 390, 4, p. 1180 (1884).

16. *People ex rel. Hastings v. Wells,* 2 California 198 at 220 (1852).

17. Harry S. Truman, see note 9, *supra;* Herbert C. Hoover to Senator Estes Kefauver, January 20, 1958; Dwight D. Eisenhower in a personal interview with the author, June 29, 1961; and Brownell, "Presidential Disability," p. 199.

18. Wickersham, "Presidential Inability," p. 288.

19. *Ibid.,* p. 262.

20. Noel Dowling, "Executive Disability," *New Hampshire Bar Journal,* I (1959), 18.

21. Harry S. Truman, article for the North American Newspaper Alliance (1957). See note 9 *supra.*

22. Max Farrand (ed.), *The Records of the Federal Convention of 1787* (New Haven: Yale University Press, 1911), II, 612. I am indebted to Mr. Katzenbach of Attorney General Kennedy's staff for bringing this quote to my attention.

23. Brownell, "Presidential Disability," p. 199.

24. Herbert Hoover to Senator Estes Kefauver, January 20, 1958, cited *Hearings, Senate Subcommittee on Constitutional Amendments,* 85th Cong., 2nd Sess. (1958), p. 11.

25. Harry S. Truman, article for the North American Newspaper Alliance (1957). See note 9 *supra*.

26. Herbert Hoover to Senator Estes Kefauver. See note 24 *supra*.

27. Silva, *Presidential Succession*, p. 108.

28. Allan Nevins, *Grover Cleveland: A Study in Courage* (New York: Dodd, Mead & Co., 1948), p. 533.

29. Michael Reilly, *Reilly of the White House* (New York: Simon & Schuster, 1947), p. 14.

30. Merriman Smith to Richard H. Hansen, September 16, 1961.

31. Sherman Adams to Richard H. Hansen, April 6, 1961.

32. Brownell, "Presidential Disability," p. 198.

33. Herbert Brownell to Richard H. Hansen, May 22, 1961.

34. Harry S. Truman, article for the North American Newspaper Alliance (1957). See note 9 *supra*.

35. Fred Blumenthal, "A Working Week-End with the President," *Parade*, April 8, 1962, p. 11.

Bibliography

The basic bibliography on presidential inability materials was prepared by Ruth Silva and can be found on pages 189–196 of *Presidential Succession* (copyright, University of Michigan, Ann Arbor, 1951). The following list supplements her compilation and extends it through July, 1962.

A. General and Special Works

ADAMS, SHERMAN. *Firsthand Report: The Story of the Eisenhower Administration.* New York: Harper and Bros., 1961.

BEMIS, SAMUEL FLAGG (ed.). *The American Secretaries of State and Their Diplomacy.* New York: Alfred A. Knopf, 1929.

CORWIN, EDWARD S. *The President: Office and Powers.* 4th rev. ed. New York: New York University Press, 1957.

CRAWFORD, THERON CLARK. *James G. Blaine: A Study of His Life and Career.* Philadelphia: J. C. Winston & Company, Inc., 1893.

DANIELS, JOSEPHUS. *The Wilson Era: Years of War and After.* Chapel Hill: University of North Carolina Press, 1946.

———. *The Life of Woodrow Wilson, 1856–1924.* Philadelphia: John C. Winston Co., 1924.

GUNTHER, JOHN. *Roosevelt in Retrospect: A Profile in History.* New York: Harper & Bros., 1950.

HOOVER, HERBERT. *The Ordeal of Woodrow Wilson.* New York: McGraw-Hill Book Co., 1958.

JOSEPHSON, EMMANUEL M. *The Strange Death of Franklin D. Roosevelt.* New York: Chedney Press, 1948.

KEEN, WILLIAM W. *The Surgical Operations on President Cleveland in 1893.* Philadelphia: George W. Jacobs & Co., 1917.

LEAHY, WILLIAM D. *I Was There.* New York: Whittlesey House, 1950.

MARSHALL, THOMAS R. *Recollections of Thomas R. Marshall.* Indianapolis: Bobbs-Merrill Co., c. 1925.

MARX, RUDOLPH, M.D. *The Health of the Presidents.* New York: G. P. Putnam's Sons, 1960.

MEANS, GASTON B. *The Strange Death of President Harding.* New York: Guild Publishing Co., 1930.

MORGAN, ROBERT J. *A Whig Embattled.* Lincoln: University of Nebraska Press, 1954.

NEVINS, ALLAN. *Grover Cleveland—a Study in Courage*. New York: Dodd, Mead & Co., 1933.

NIXON, RICHARD M. *Six Crises*. Garden City: Doubleday & Co., Inc., 1962.

PERKINS, FRANCES. *The Roosevelt I Knew*. New York: The Viking Press, 1946.

REILLY, MICHAEL F. *Reilly of the White House* (as told to WILLIAM J. SLOCUM). New York: Simon & Schuster, 1947.

ROBINSON, EDGAR EUGENE. *The Roosevelt Leadership, 1933–1945*. Philadelphia: J. B. Lippincott Co., 1955.

ROOSEVELT, JAMES (with SIDNEY SHALLETT). *Affectionately, F.D.R.: A Son's Story of a Lonely Man*. New York: Harcourt, Brace and Co., 1959.

ROSENMAN, SAMUEL I. *Working with Roosevelt*. New York: Harper & Bros., 1952.

SHERWOOD, ROBERT E. *Roosevelt and Hopkins: An Intimate History*. New York: Harper & Bros., 1948.

SILVA, RUTH. *Presidential Succession*. Ann Arbor: University of Michigan Press, 1951.

STETTINIUS, EDWARD R., JR. *Roosevelt and the Russians: The Yalta Conference*, ed. WALTER JOHNSON. Garden City: Doubleday & Co., Inc., 1949.

TRUMAN, HARRY S. *Memoirs*, 2 vols. Garden City: Doubleday & Co., Inc., 1955.

———. *Mr. Citizen*. New York: Bernard Geis Associates, 1960.

TULLY, GRACE. *F.D.R., My Boss*. New York: Charles Scribner's Sons, 1949.

WAUGH, EDGAR W. *Second Consul*. Indianapolis: Bobbs-Merrill & Co., 1956.

WILLIAMS, IRVING G. *The Rise of the Vice Presidency*. New York: Public Affairs Press, 1956.

WOLD, KARL C., M.D. *Mr. President—How Is Your Health?* Milwaukee: Bruce Publishing Co., 1948.

B. *Selected Articles*

ADAMS, SHERMAN. "Critical Days of Ike's Three Illnesses" (excerpt from memoirs), *Life*, L (May 26, 1961), 92–94.

———. "What Goes on in the White House When the President Is Sick" (excerpts from address, December 9, 1957), *U. S. News and World Report*, XLIII (December 20, 1957), 88–89.

BARTHOLOMEW, PAUL C. "Summary View: The Problem of

Presidential Disability," *American Bar Association Journal*, XLIV (June, 1958), 542.

BLUMENTHAL, FRED. "A Working Week-End with the President," *Parade*, April 8, 1962.

BROWNELL, HERBERT, JR. "Presidential Disability: The Need for a Constitutional Amendment," *Yale Law Journal*, LXVIII (1958), 189–211.

CELLER, EMMANUEL (M. C.). Problem of Presidential Inability," *Federal Rules Digest*, XIX (August, 1956), 153.

CLARKE, MARY M. "Who Would Succeed?" *America*, LXXXXV (August 25, 1956), 483–485.

DEUTSCH, MONROE E. "Veeps Can Become Presidents," *Nation*, CLXXV (December 20, 1952), 579–580. Reply: WILMERDING, LUCIUS, JR. *Ibid.*, CLXXVI (February 14, 1953), 155.

DOUB, GEORGE C. "Presidential Disability" (address, May 25, 1959), *Vital Speeches*, XXV (September 1, 1959), 702–704.

———. "Presidential Inability: The Constitutional Problem" (address), *Maine State Bar Association*, XLVIII (1959), 186.

DOWLING, NOEL T. "Executive Disability," *New Hampshire Bar Journal*, I (January, 1959), 14–18.

EISENHOWER, DWIGHT D. "How the President Views the Outlook for a Tax Cut" (excerpts from a news conference, April 3, 1957), *U. S. News and World Report*, XLII (April 12, 1957), 110–111.

FOLLIARD, EDWARD T. "Washington Mood: Presidency as a Mankiller," *Nation's Business*, XLVI (October, 1958), 27–28.

FRELINGHUYSEN, PETER, JR. "Presidential Disability," *Annals of the American Academy of Political and Social Science*, CCCVII (September, 1956), 144–155.

GASPIRINI, EDWIN L. "Presidential Inability Riddle," *New York State Bar Bulletin*, XXXI (July, 1959), 258.

GILLIAM, ARMISTEAD W., and SLOAT, JONATHAN W. "Presidential Inability," *George Washington University Law Review*, XXIV (March, 1956), 448–464.

GOULD, KENNETH M. "When a President Is Ill," *Scholastic*, LXVII (October 20, 1955), 13.

GREEN, THEODORE F. (Sen.). "Presidential Succession," *Dickinson Law Review*, LXI (June, 1957), 323.

HANSEN, RICHARD H. "Executive Disability: A Void in State and Federal Law," *Nebraska Law Review*, XL (June, 1961), 697.

———. "One Strike and You're Out: The Constitution and Executive Disability," *New Hampshire Bar Journal*, IV (October, 1962).

HAZLITT, HENRY. "To Remove Uncertainty," *Newsweek*, L (December 16, 1957), 105.

———. "Vice Presidency," *Newsweek*, XLIX (April 15, 1957), 101.

HEINLEIN, J. C. "Problem of Presidential Inability," *University of Cincinnati Law Review*, XXV (Summer, 1956), 310.

HYMAN, SYDNEY. "The Founding Fathers and Presidential Disability," *Reporter*, XIII (October 20, 1955), 11–12.

———. "Issue of Presidential Disability," *New York Times Magazine*, February 26, 1956, p. 13.

JOHNSON, GERALD W. "Inability Pact," *New Republic*, CXXXVIII (March 17, 1958), 10.

———. "Long Example," *New Republic*, CXLI (August 10, 1959), 18.

———. "Presidential Disability," *New Republic*, CXXXVI (April 29, 1957), 8.

KNEBEL, FLETCHER. "On the Spot: The President's Doctor," *Look*, XX (September 18, 1956), 88.

KOONCE, DAVID. "What the Constitution Doesn't Tell Us: Who Shall Determine if a President Is Disabled?" *Democratic Digest*, III (June, 1956), 57–59.

MOLEY, RAYMOND. "Lilliputian Regency," *Newsweek*, L (December 16, 1957), 124.

———. "No Time for Committees," *Newsweek*, L (December 9, 1957), 108.

MORLEY, F. "Presidential Succession: A Problem Congress Has to Face," *Nation's Business*, XLIII (December, 1955), 17–18.

MURROW and FRIENDLY. *I Can Hear It Now*, Vol. III, 1919–1932. Columbia Records, Inc. (1950).

PARSONS, WILFRID. "Who Shall Succeed, and How?" *America*, LXXXXVIII (March 15, 1958), 686.

———. "Who Succeeds a Disabled President?" *America*, LXXXXVI (April 6, 1957), 6.

ROBERTS, CHARLES. "Keeping the President Fit," *Newsweek*, XLIX (June 24, 1957), 63–65.

ROGERS, WILLIAM P. "Presidential Inability" (address, April 25, 1958), *Vital Speeches*, XXIV (July 1, 1958), 568–570.

ROOSEVELT, ELLIOTT. "They're Lying about F.D.R.'s Health," *Liberty*, May, 1949, p. 76.

RUTSTEIN, DAVID D., M.D. "Doctors and Politics," *Atlantic Monthly*, CLXXXXVIII (August, 1956), 32–35.

SILVA, RUTH C. "Presidential Inability," *University of Detroit Law Journal*, XXXV (December, 1957), 139.

———. "Presidential Succession and Disability," *Law and Contemporary Problems*, XXI (1956), 646.

SMITH, BEVERLY, JR. "If a President Collapses," *Saturday Evening Post*, CCXXIX (March 23, 1957), 20–21.

STAFFORD, JANE. "Top Level Medical Care," *Science News Letter*, LXIX (February 11, 1956), 90–91.

TRUMAN, HARRY S. "Presidential Disability," *New York Times*, June 24, 1957, p. 1, col. 3.

WALLACE, HENRY A. "How a Vice President Is Picked" (address), *U. S. News and World Report*, XL (April 6, 1956), 86–89.

WHARTON, DON. "If a President Becomes Disabled," *Readers Digest*, LXXI (November, 1957), 52–55.

WICKERSHAM, CORNELIUS W. "Presidential Inability: Procrastination, Apathy and the Constitution," *Villanova Law Review*, VII (Winter, 1961–1962), 262.

WILMERDING, LUCIUS, JR. "Presidential Inability," *Political Science Quarterly*, LXXII (1957), 161–181.

WOLD, KARL C., M.D. "The Truth about F.D.R.'s Health," *Look*, February 15, 1949.

WYMAN, LOUIS C. "When a President Is Too Ill to Handle the Job: Precedent in New Hampshire," *U. S. News and World Report*, XL (March 9, 1956), 44–45.

C. *Selected Notes and Comments*

"Administration Asks Constitutional Rules for Replacing a Disabled President," *Business Week*, April 6, 1957, p. 151.

"Constitution Is Vague, and Brownell Describes the Situation as Reckless," *Life*, XLIII (December 9, 1957), 36–39.

"Dangerous Oversight," *Newsweek*, XLVII (March 12, 1956), 29.

"End to Disability Puzzle?" *Senior Scholastic*, LXXII (March 21, 1958), 17.

"For Emergency Use Only: Substitute President," *Senior Scholastic*, LXX (April 19, 1957), 14–16.

"How Old Is Too Old to Become President?" *U. S. News and World Report*, XXXIX (August 26, 1955), 22–25.

"If Illness Does Disable Ike," *U. S. News and World Report*, XLIII (December 6, 1957), 38–40.

"If Nixon Became an Acting President, with Views of President Eisenhower," *U. S. News and World Report*, XLIV (March 14, 1958), 75–78.

"If the President Dies . . . Pro and Con Discussion," *Scholastic*, LXXI (December 10, 1952), 7–9.

"If the President Is Disabled: What Ike Has Told Nixon," *U. S. News and World Report*, XLIV (March 7, 1958), 33–35.

"Ike's Course; Nixon's Niche," *Newsweek*, L (December 9, 1957), 27–34.

"Line of Succession," *Time*, LX (November 24, 1952), 21.

"Minor Ailment," *Time*, LXXVI (June 23, 1961), 9–10.

"Must Item for the Next Congress," *Business Week*, December 7, 1957, p. 184.

"Nixon's Responsibiltiy," *New Republic*, CXXXVI (April 15, 1957), 3. Reply: PETER FREYLINGHUYSEN, JR., *Ibid.*, CCCXXXVI (April 22, 1957), 6–7.

"Nonsense, or Not?" *Newsweek*, XLIX (April 8, 1957), 30–31.

"On Disability, Let's Have Action," *Life*, XLIV (February 24, 1958), 32.

"One Hundred Seventy Year Old Riddle," *Time*, LXX (December 9, 1957), 23.

"Operation Candor," *Reporter*, XIV (March 22, 1956), 2.

"Presidential Disability," *Commonweal*, LXVI (April 19, 1957), 53.

"Presidential Inability: The Problem and a Recommendation," *George Washington University Law Review*, XXIV (March, 1956), 448.

"Presidents and Their Health," *U. S. News and World Report*, XL (March 9, 1956), 50–52.

"President's Disability and Succession," *St. John's Law Review*, XXXII (May, 1958), 357.

"Question of Adequate Legal Provision for Presidential Disability, Pro and Con," *Congressional Digest*, XXXVII (January, 1958), 1–32.

"Sherman Adams Says It," *Newsweek*, L (December 16, 1957), 35.

"Should Mr. Eisenhower Resign?" *Commonweal*, LXVII (December 20, 1957), 299.

"Substitute President," *Senior Scholastic*, LXX (April 12, 1957), 19.

"Succession Agreement," *Time*, LXXI (March 10, 1958), 12.

"Vital Precedent," *Time*, LXXI (March 17, 1958), 14.

"Washington Outlook: Eisenhower-Nixon Pact," *Business Week*, March 8, 1958, p. 39.

"We Need a Plan for the Relief of Ailing Presidents," *Saturday Evening Post*, CCXXIX (March 23, 1957), 10.

"We've Been Asked, if a President-Elect Dies——," *U. S. News and World Report*, III (November 14, 1952), 84.

"What Mr. Sam Wants," *Time*, LXXI (March 24, 1958), 24.

"When a President Is Disabled," *U. S. News and World Report*, XLII (April 5, 1957), 34–35.

"When Presidents Become Ill There's No Clear Line of Authority," *U. S. News and World Report*, XXXIX (October 7, 1955), 60–63.

"Who Decides When?" *Newsweek*, LI (February 17, 1958), 27.

"Who Gets the Power When a President Is Disabled?" *U. S. News and World Report*, XL (June 15, 1956), 69–70.

D. Selected Documentary Materials

Annual Report, American Bar Association, 1960, p. 129.

Hearings before Special Subcommittee of House Committee on the Judiciary to Study Presidential Inability, 84th Congress, Second Session, 1956.

Hearings before a Special Subcommittee on the Study of Presidential Inability of the House Committee on the Judiciary, 85th Congress, First Session, 1957.

Hearings before the Subcommittee on Constitutional Amendments of the Senate Judiciary Committee, 85th Congress, First Session, 1958.

Letters of Grover Cleveland, 1850–1908, selected and edited by ALLAN NEVINS. Boston: Houghton-Mifflin and Company, 1933.

Opinions of the Attorneys General, Vol. XLII, No. 5 (August 2, 1961).

"Presidential Inability," *House Committee Print, Commit-*

tee on the Judiciary, House of Representatives, January 31, 1956, 84th Congress, Second Session.

"Presidential Inability," *House Committee Print,* 85th Congress, First Session.

"Presidential Inability Report," *New York State Bar Bulletin,* XXIX (April, 1957), 108–110.

"A Report on the Problem of Presidential Inability," *Committee on Federal Legislation: Association of the Bar of the City of New York,* I (May, 1962), 51–69.

"Report of Committee on the Federal Constitution," *New York State Bar Association, Proceedings* (1957), pp. 147–148.

"Report of the Standing Committee on Jurisprudence and Law Reform," *American Bar Association Proceedings,* LXXXV (1961), 175–176.

Acknowledgments

The unstinting cooperation of many people has made this book possible. First of all, my thanks must go to former Presidents Dwight D. Eisenhower and Harry S. Truman for their time, their counsel, and their unfailing kindness. I am deeply grateful to Don H. Sherwood, Richard A. Peterson, Charles M. Pallesen, Jr., Richard H. Shugrue, and Professor Robert Hepburn for their invaluable assistance and encouragement; to the University of Nebraska Press for suggesting the plan of this book and for additional research on historical background; and to Dr. Ruth Silva, whose *Presidential Succession* is indispensable to any student of presidential inability.

Special thanks are due to Mrs. Ann Whitman, Secretary to General Eisenhower, and Miss Rose Conway, Secretary to former President Truman. Merriman Smith, dean of the White House press corps, was kind enough to visit with me a number of times and to write several passages for this book.

Various members of the Kennedy Administration have been extremely helpful: Theodore C. Sorensen, Special Counsel to President Kennedy; Nicholas deB. Katzenbach, Deputy Attorney General of the United States; Harold F. Reis, Acting Assistant Attorney General of the United States, Office of Legal Counsel; and the Hon. Adlai E. Stevenson, United States Ambassador to the United Nations. Mr. Stevenson's aunt, Mrs. Julia Hardin, daughter of Vice President Adlai Stevenson, graciously wrote an account of the relationship between the Stevenson and Cleveland families while President Cleveland was in office.

Members of General Eisenhower's Administration were also extremely cooperative in making materials available and in giving their comments on the various proposals. I am particularly indebted to former Attorney General Herbert Brownell and to Sherman Adams, former Assistant to the President.

Certain members of Congress, among them Senator Estes Kefauver, have been generous with their time and advice. The late Speaker of the House Sam Rayburn gave his assistance on two occasions. It is impossible to forget the kindness of Robert J. Kutak, Legislative Assistant to Senator Roman Hruska of Nebraska; James C. Kirby, Jr., Chief Counsel to the Senate Subcommittee on Constitutional Amendments; the late Senator Styles Bridges of New Hampshire; and Bernard J. Waters, Minority Counsel, Senate Subcommittee on Constitutional Rights.

I should also like to express my thanks to the following people who responded to queries or were helpful in other ways: former Vice President Richard M. Nixon; Cornelius W. Wickersham; Louis C. Wyman, Chairman of the Standing Committee on Jurisprudence and Law Reform of the American Bar Association; Thomas E. Dewey; Mrs. Franklin D. Roosevelt; Rudolph Marx, M.D.; Robert L. Oshins, Director of Research, Democratic National Committee, and William B. Prendergast, Director of Research, Republican National Committee; Mr. Justice Tom C. Clark of the United States Supreme Court; John Patterson, Governor of Alabama; Edward L. Fossett, Administrative Assistant to Governor Combs of Kentucky; Bradford H. Hutchins, Republican National Committeeman for the state of Maine; J. E. Springmeyer, Legislative Counsel for the state of Nevada; Grant Sawyer, Governor of the state of Nevada; Edwin L. Mechen, Governor of New Mexico; Frank Wille, Assistant Counsel to Governor Rockefeller of New York; William L. Guy, Governor of North Dakota; Leslie Burgum, Attorney General of North Dakota; J. Howard Edmondson, Governor of Oklahoma; Mark O. Hatfield, Governor of Oregon; Otis B. Morse, Secretary to Governor Lawrence of Pennsylvania; Archie Gubbrud, Governor of South Dakota; C. L. Chase, Democratic National Committeeman for South Dakota; Ross W. Dyer, Executive Assistant to Governor Buford Ellington of Tennessee; Price Daniel, Governor of Texas; George D. Clyde, Governor of Utah; F. Ray Keyser, Jr., Governor of Vermont; J. Lindsay Almond, Jr., Governor of Virginia; Robert D. Timm, Republican National Committeeman from the state of Washington; Albert D. Rosellini, Governor of Washington; and Alfred M. Landon, former Governor of Kansas.

While I am happy to acknowledge my debt to the many persons listed here, it is with the full recognition that all errors or shortcomings in this book are wholly my own.

Finally, special thanks to my wife, who has shared in this undertaking in all its phases from beginning to end.

RICHARD H. HANSEN

Index